Port Washington Public Library

Port Washington, New York

Phone: 883-4400

APR 13 1988

PW Fi

The Incredible Journey of Lewis and Clark

RHODA BLUMBERG

▲ ▲ ▲

The Incredible Journey of Lewis and Clark

Lothrop, Lee & Shepard Books · New York

*I am grateful for the expert advice and guidance
of Dr. James P. Ronda, Professor of History
at Youngstown State University, Youngstown, Ohio.*

TITLE PAGE ILLUSTRATION: Sacred circles of buffalo skulls were used
to mark Sun Dance ceremonies, the most holy of Plains Indian
rituals. Although this painting shows circles on the upper Platte
River, Lewis and Clark saw many similar ones on their journey.

Maps on pages 10–11, 14, 23, and 110–111 © 1987 by Mike Eagle

First Edition 1 2 3 4 5 6 7 8 9 10

Library of Congress Cataloging in Publication Data
Blumberg, Rhoda. The incredible journey of Lewis and Clark.
Bibliography: p.   Includes index. Summary: Describes the expedition led by Lewis and Clark to
explore the unknown western regions of America at the beginning of the nineteenth century.
1. Lewis and Clark Expedition (1804–1806)—Juvenile literature.   2. Lewis, Meriwether,
1774–1809—Juvenile literature.   3. Clark, William, 1770–1838—Juvenile literature.   4. West
(U.S.)—Description and travel—To 1848—Juvenile literature.   [1. Lewis and Clark Expedition
(1804–1806)   2. Lewis, Meriwether, 1774–1809.   3. Clark, William, 1770–1838.   4. Explorers.
5. West (U.S.)—Discovery and exploration]   I. Title.
F592.7.B55   1987   917.8′042   87-4235
ISBN 0-688-06512-0

For
Daniel, Carla, Ilana
William, Melodica
Gregory, Amalia
Dana

BY RHODA BLUMBERG

Commodore Perry in the Land of the Shogun

Contents

A group of dome-shaped clay bluffs on the Missouri River

FOREWORD

When young Sergeant John Ordway was ready to head west with the Lewis and Clark expedition in May 1804, he wrote to his parents about the "Great Discoveries" the explorers expected to make. Two and one-half years and seven thousand miles later, a seasoned Ordway quietly put the last entry in a journal he had kept each day. After all the wonders of the Great West, it was time "to See our parents once more as we have been so long from them."

The sergeant did not make a list of the "Great Discoveries" accomplished in years of wilderness travel. He would leave that to Meriwether Lewis and William Clark. And what a list it was! Every river twist, all the trail turns, each range of mountains had been carefully mapped. Expedition journals were filled with descriptions of plants, animals, and native peoples. Packs bulged with specimens tagged for study by eager scientists in Philadelphia.

All of this was the result of precise instructions to Lewis and Clark from President Thomas Jefferson. The president wanted his explorers to do more than take a grand western sightseeing tour. The expedition was ordered to hold

THE INCREDIBLE JOURNEY OF LEWIS & CLARK

meetings with western Indians while at the same time studying their cultures. Lewis and Clark were assigned important scientific duties ranging from gathering plant and animal samples to keeping accurate records of mountain weather. And of course, Jefferson hoped his captains would find profitable trade routes, by navigable rivers if possible, to link East and West. In doing all this, Lewis and Clark inched the West from fantasies about mountains made of salt and plains full of volcanoes to the realities of science and business. The expedition marked the young nation's first western venture. More than a daring enterprise, the Lewis and Clark expedition was a journey that produced knowledge—knowledge to spark the minds of scientists and fire the imaginations of restless settlers.

Rhoda Blumberg's *The Incredible Journey of Lewis and Clark* is not just a simple retelling of a familiar story. The book draws upon the most recent expedition scholarship to explain the many complex missions carried out by the explorers. It dramatizes what it meant for the explorers to be geographers, zoologists, diplomats, and students of Indian life. Ms. Blumberg brings alive the awe Lewis and Clark felt when they saw plains black with buffalo, rock towers twisted in mysterious shapes, and snowy mountains stretching beyond the western horizon. But throughout this serious exploration, we are always reminded that the expedition was also an amazing adventure. Ms. Blumberg puts us alongside Lewis and Clark as they struggled up the Missouri River, searched for Rocky Mountain passes, and nearly froze in the bitter snows of the Lolo Trail.

When the young Shoshoni woman Sacagawea reached the West Coast with the expedition, she was not among the first of the group to see the Pacific Ocean. Sacagawea complained, saying she "had traveled a long way . . . to see the great waters." She got her wish. Like her, all of us want to see the "great waters." We want to share in the continuing rediscovery of our western heritage. Rhoda Blumberg takes us on that voyage. She brings us to a West as wide as the imagination, a West of destiny for all Americans.

JAMES P. RONDA
Professor of History
Department of History
Youngstown State University

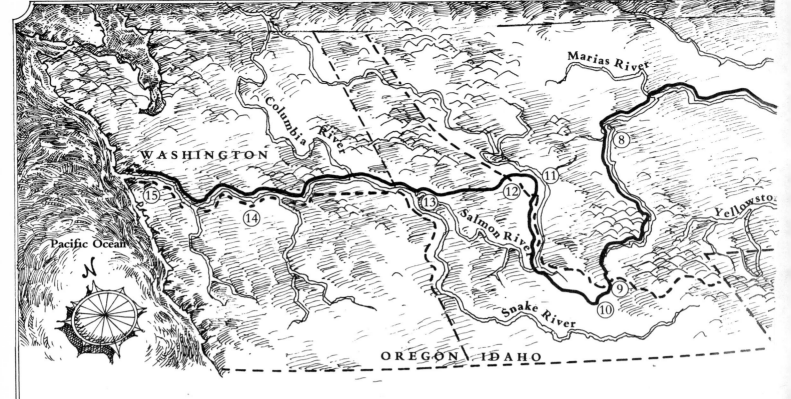

THE JOURNEY WEST (ABOVE)

1. Camp Wood December 11, 1803–May 12, 1804. Camped here while preparing for journey. (pages 25–32)

2. St. Charles May 16–20, 1804. Expedition waited here for Lewis, who remained briefly in St. Louis. (pages 32–34)

3. Council Bluff August 3, 1804. Meeting with Missouri and Oto Indians. (pages 38–39)

4. Calumet Bluff August 28–September 1, 1804. Held council with Yankton Sioux August 30–31. (page 50)

5. Bad River September 25, 1804. Held council with Teton Sioux. (pages 51–53)

6. Arikara Campsite October 12, 1804. Held council with Arikaras. (pages 56–60)

7. Mandan and Hidatsa Villages October 27, 1804–April 7, 1805. Expedition built Fort Mandan and spent the winter with the Mandan and Hidatsa Indians. (pages 61–76)

8. Great Falls June 13–July 14, 1805. Camped here to doctor the sick and prepare 18-mile portage. (pages 84–85)

9. Continental Divide August 12, 1805. (page 88)

10. With the Shoshonis August 13–30, 1805. (pages 89–92)

11. Traveler's Rest September 9–11, 1805. (page 94)

12. Lolo Trail September 11–20, 1805. Path used to cross the Bitterroot Mountains. (pages 94–95)

13. Canoe Camp September 24–October 7, 1805. Expedition's camp near Nez Perce Indians. (pages 96–97)

14. Celilo Falls and Dalles Falls October 23–25, 1805. (pages 101–102)

15. Fort Clatsop December 7, 1805–March 23, 1806. Expedition's winter quarters on the Netul River. (pages 106–109)

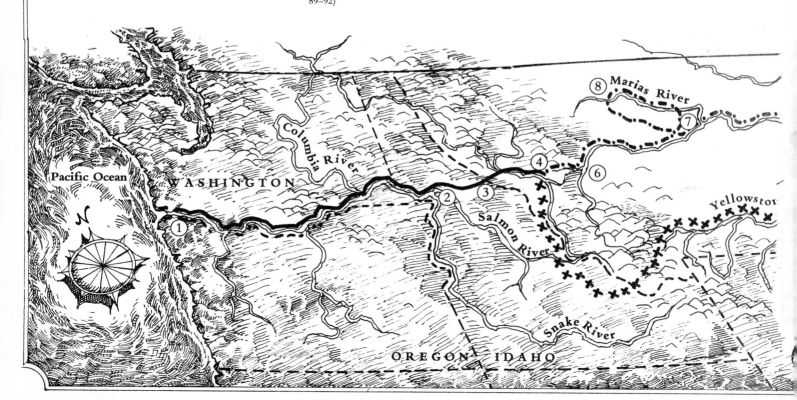

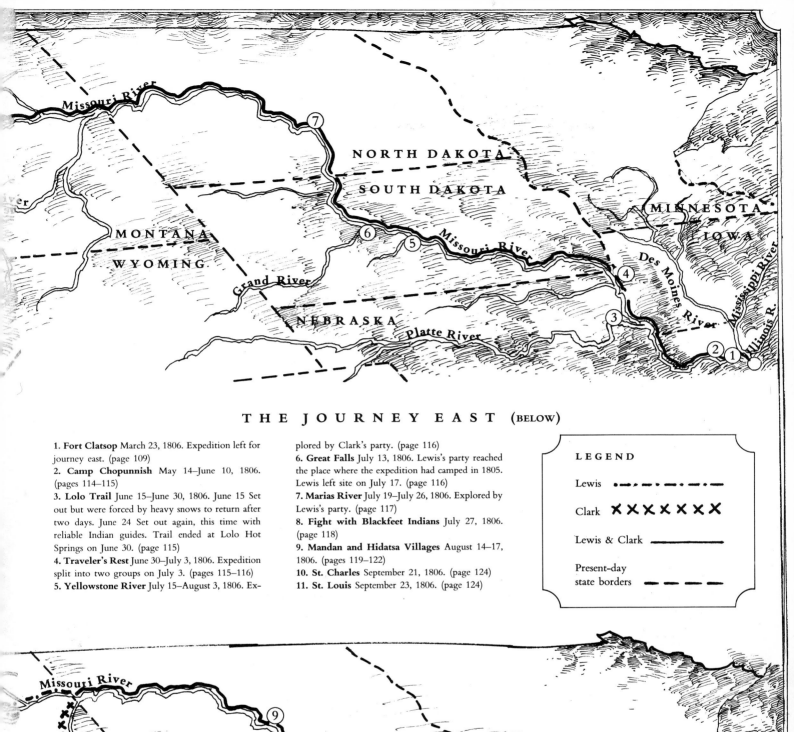

THE JOURNEY EAST (BELOW)

1. Fort Clatsop March 23, 1806. Expedition left for journey east. (page 109)

2. Camp Chopunnish May 14–June 10, 1806. (pages 114–115)

3. Lolo Trail June 15–June 30, 1806. June 15 Set out but were forced by heavy snows to return after two days. June 24 Set out again, this time with reliable Indian guides. Trail ended at Lolo Hot Springs on June 30. (page 115)

4. Traveler's Rest June 30–July 3, 1806. Expedition split into two groups on July 3. (pages 115–116)

5. Yellowstone River July 15–August 3, 1806. Ex-

plored by Clark's party. (page 116)

6. Great Falls July 13, 1806. Lewis's party reached the place where the expedition had camped in 1805. Lewis left site on July 17. (page 116)

7. Marias River July 19–July 26, 1806. Explored by Lewis's party. (page 117)

8. Fight with Blackfeet Indians July 27, 1806. (page 118)

9. Mandan and Hidatsa Villages August 14–17, 1806. (pages 119–122)

10. St. Charles September 21, 1806. (page 124)

11. St. Louis September 23, 1806. (page 124)

LEGEND

Lewis ·—··—··—··—·

Clark ✕✕✕✕✕✕✕

Lewis & Clark ————————

Present-day state borders – – – – – –

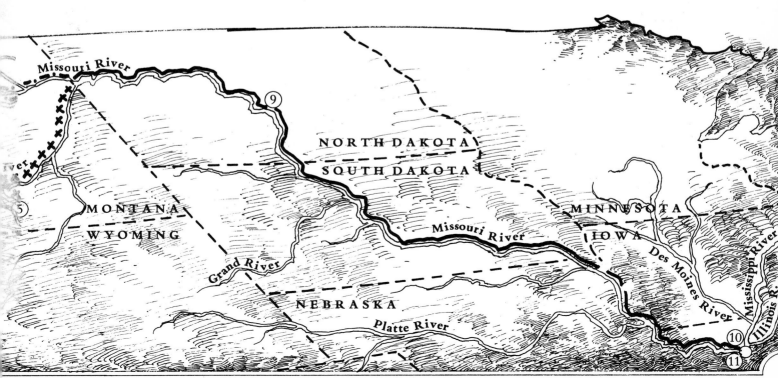

Thomas Jefferson, President of the United States, 1801–1809

1·Top Secret

AN EXPEDITION INTO MYSTERIOUS LANDS beyond the boundaries of the United States!

American explorers would cross the nation's western border—the Mississippi River—then paddle, row, and sail their way across the middle of the continent to the Pacific Ocean. The Mississippi, Missouri, and Columbia Rivers would act as one continuous waterway. If the Missouri didn't connect with the Columbia, the explorers would carry their canoes for a short distance, from one river to another.

President Thomas Jefferson proposed this expedition in a secret message to Congress on January 18, 1803. Jefferson's ideas didn't sound ridiculous because at that time many scientists were certain that these major American rivers flowed into one another.

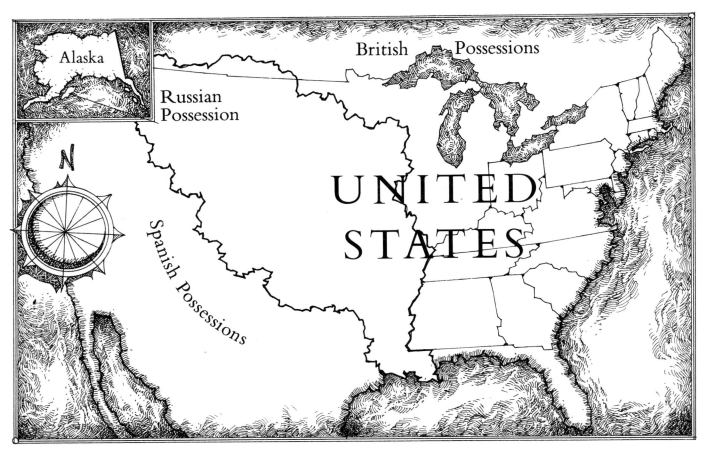

The United States and foreign possessions, about 1804

In 1803, most of the West was as mysterious as Mars. It was an uncharted, blank space on all maps. Distances were underestimated and deserts unknown. People weren't even aware of the enormous height and width of the Rocky Mountains.

Foreign powers were competing for lands west of the Mississippi. Spain had stretched her Mexican borders north, and west to California. France owned a vast area on the west side of the Mississippi, just across from United States territory. Russia, having colonized Alaska, had an eye on the California coast. England posed the gravest threat. Even though the colonists had won the American Revolution in 1783, the British still had forts and trading posts on United

THE INCREDIBLE JOURNEY OF LEWIS & CLARK

States territory in 1803. Their trappers and traders worked south of the Great Lakes, where they monopolized trade with the Indians, bartering goods and guns for furs.

Thomas Jefferson was especially alarmed after reading a book by Alexander Mackenzie, a Scottish fur trader who had crossed Canada and reached the Pacific Ocean in 1793. In his book, *Voyages from Montreal,* Mackenzie urged the British government to set up forts and trading posts across the continent and along the Pacific coast.

Jefferson was convinced that a United States expedition was urgent. The Americans must prevent the English from

Trapping beaver was an important industry in the 1800s.

Beaver on the Missouri

claiming new territories on the American continent.[1] In his message to Congress, the President didn't mention the nation's need to control the continent. Congressmen were probably expected to read between the lines. Jefferson merely stated that an expedition was necessary for "extending the external commerce of the United States."[2]

Commerce was indeed one of Jefferson's important goals. Trapping and trading for furs were important to the nation's economy. By winning the West, the United States would find new sources of furs. American pelts were sold not only in Europe but also in Asia. Sea captains from America's East Coast enjoyed a fabulously profitable trade with China, where they bartered furs and other items for tea, silks, and porcelains (known as "chinaware").

However, to reach the Orient, Yankee skippers had to travel around South America, endangering their ships in the treacherous waters of Cape Horn.

If Jefferson's expedition provided a shortcut across America, eastern merchants could send their cargoes to and from the Pacific by river. Then, ships docked and waiting on the West Coast could sail to and from the Orient.

In addition to political and commercial aims, the President expected the explorers to contribute new information about nature and native American people.

Jefferson referred to his proposed expedition as a "literary pursuit." By "literary," he meant *scientific;* by "pursuit," *quest for knowledge.* He realized that some Senators and Congressmen mocked his ideas and viewed the West as a worthless wasteland. Therefore, he asked Congress for only $2,500 to finance his "Voyage of Discovery." The low estimate guaranteed that political opponents would not veto his proposal. The President assured Congress that his mission could be accomplished by "an intelligent officer with ten or twelve chosen men."[3]

THE INCREDIBLE JOURNEY OF LEWIS & CLARK

2·An Intelligent Officer

THE "INTELLIGENT OFFICER" chosen to command Jefferson's "literary pursuit" was Meriwether Lewis. Lewis was twenty-eight years old and had served as the President's personal secretary for two years. Lewis had never attended college, but he had received a superb education at the White House with Jefferson. Lewis used the President's extensive library, which had books on a staggering number of subjects, ranging from astronomy to zoology.

Jefferson declared that politics was his "duty," but natural history his "passion."[1] He conveyed this passion to Lewis, and boasted that his secretary had developed a talent for observing plants and animals.

Lewis helped the President plot a cross-country exploration. Although Jefferson had never been more than fifty miles west of Monticello, Virginia, he expected to advise and guide his secretary through an unknown wilderness. The President even invented a secret code, to be used whenever he and Lewis corresponded. Messengers were supposed to find their way to and from Washington, D.C., with reports that only Lewis and Jefferson could decipher. The White

Meriwether Lewis

House would act as a control center for adventurers in unknown space. The code, however, was never used. It turned out to be impossible to dispatch messengers from the western wilderness to Washington.

Expert Advice

To prepare Lewis for the great expedition, Jefferson sent his secretary to see scholars in Philadelphia. In one month, Lewis was given cram courses in science. The botanist Benjamin

Smith Barton taught him the art of preserving plants and furnished notes on zoology and Indian history. The astronomer Caspar Wistar talked not only about constellations, but about fossils as well. He urged Lewis to collect bones and warned him to watch out for living mammoths—and for "Great Claw" (a giant sloth). It was possible, he claimed, that these monsters might be roaming about in the uncharted West.

Dr. Benjamin Rush, the country's outstanding physician, assembled a medicine kit and gave Lewis implements for bleeding and operating on patients. He also supplied fifty dozen of his own pills—laxatives that were to become known as "Rush's thunderbolts."

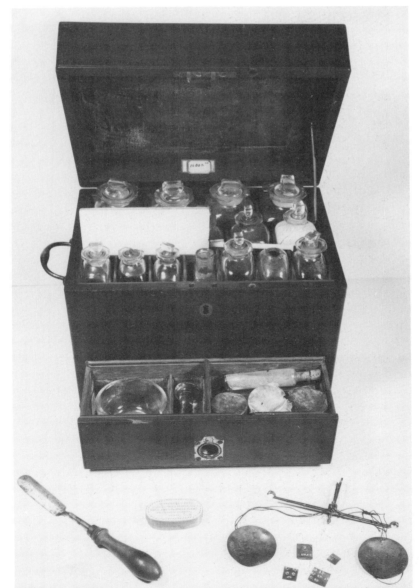

Medicine chest owned by Dr. Benjamin Rush, who assembled a similar kit for the expedition.

19

Because the explorers would have to doctor themselves, Rush also supplied written rules "for the Preservation of his [Lewis's] Health and of those who were to accompany him":

· When fatigued, lie down for two whole hours.
· Wash your feet in cold water every morning. [Jefferson always did!]
· When your feet are chilled wash them with "a little spirits" [liquor].
· During difficult marches eat very little to avoid becoming overtired.[2]

Dr. Benjamin Rush

Mandan medicine man. Captain Lewis was expected to study Indians' healing rituals and remedies.

Dr. Rush also prepared a lengthy questionnaire for Lewis about the health of the Indians they would meet: their diseases, remedies, eating habits, lifespans. Lewis was even expected to check the pulse rate of children and adults "in the morning, at noon, and at night before and after eating."[3]

Before leaving Philadelphia, Lewis bought over a ton of supplies that included gifts for Indians. There were beads, buttons, curtain rings (to adorn fingers and ears), ruffled shirts, red fabrics, red-handled knives, and red paint for decorating bodies. Tomahawks and knives were also included as gifts.

Camp supplies, clothing, and weapons had to be purchased. With the help of a professional cook, Lewis concocted 150 pounds of "portable soup"—a dried, instant broth that tasted terrible, but would be used if the explorers ran short of food.

Scientific instruments such as quadrants, compasses, and magnifying devices were also on the shopping list. And there were books on mineralogy, botany, history, anatomy, and astronomy that Lewis borrowed or bought. A four-volume dictionary was part of a weighty library to be lugged, round trip, from coast to coast.

Lewis designed a collapsible canoe. The boat's frame came

apart for carrying, weighed about one hundred pounds, and could be assembled easily. It was supposed to carry a ton of gear. Lewis was proud of his ingenious invention. He named his creation "The Experiment."

Wagons transported supplies and purchases to Pittsburgh, where they were loaded on a boat for shipment down the Ohio River. From there they were sent up the Mississippi to St. Louis.

Official Instructions

President Jefferson issued official instructions for Lewis. He stressed that the purpose of the expedition was to discover a direct water route to the Pacific Ocean. Lewis was also obligated to make detailed reports about soil, vegetation, fossils, minerals, climate, mammals, insects, birds, and reptiles. All observations were "to be taken with great pains & accuracy, to be entered distinctly and intelligibly" into an official log of the expedition.

The President urged Lewis to tell Indians of "our wish to be neighborly, friendly, and useful to them." He stressed that it was important to obtain the names of Indian nations, their numbers, and "the articles of trade they may need or furnish." As the ultimate goodwill gesture, Lewis was to invite Indian chiefs to visit Washington, D.C., as guests of the United States government.[4]

When Jefferson issued these official instructions on June 20, 1803, he had no idea that American diplomats in Paris had already purchased a huge chunk of North America. Napoleon sold France's Louisiana Territory at the bargain price of 15 million dollars. The great conqueror needed money for his European campaigns. This was history's greatest real estate deal. For four cents an acre, the United States doubled its size.[5]

THE INCREDIBLE JOURNEY OF LEWIS & CLARK

Louisiana Purchase, 1803

The purchase agreement was dated April 30, 1803, but the news did not reach Jefferson until July. The President was relieved. Napoleon the Great was no longer his nation's unwanted neighbor. The expedition need no longer be viewed as an undercover intelligence mission on foreign soil. The men would openly explore territory now owned by the United States. However, they would still invade no-man's land after they reached the foothills of the Rocky Mountains.

William Clark

William Clark

Faced with the challenge of leading men into the unknown, Lewis decided he wanted his friend, thirty-three-year-old William Clark, as co-leader of the expedition.

Before Lewis had been appointed Jefferson's secretary, he had served in the army with Clark. Both men had been trained by General "Mad Anthony" Wayne, a fanatic who demanded excessive inspections, drills, and discipline. Clark was an experienced woodsman, a good surveyor, and a fine leader. At one time he had been Lewis's commanding officer.

Clark had retired from the army and was managing his family's farm in Kentucky when he received the letter from Lewis asking him to become co-captain of the expedition. Eager for action, Clark replied that he looked forward to the "dangers, difficulties, and fatigues," and assured Lewis that "no man lives whith whome I perfur to undertake such a Trip as yourself."[6]

Clark's acceptance brightened for Lewis an aggravating summer spent in Pittsburgh. He was waiting for boatbuilders ("incorrigible drunkards") who took their time completing a fifty-five-foot barge with sails, called a keelboat.

Lewis was so impatient to get going that on August 31, 1803, only four hours after the long-overdue boat was finished, he launched it down the Ohio. Half a dozen recruits from the army, a river pilot, and three men whose qualifications were "on trial" accompanied him. Clark, Clark's slave, York, and more volunteer soldiers came aboard at Louisville, Kentucky.

Drought had made the water level of the Ohio River so low that horses or oxen frequently had to be hired to pull the boat across shoals. From the Ohio, the boat turned up the Mississippi, and the men set up Camp Wood eighteen miles from the small town of St. Louis.

3·Getting Ready

SPANISH OFFICIALS were disturbed by the presence of the expedition on the Mississippi. They wrote to one another denouncing "Captain Merry and his followers." They were sure that "Mr. Merry" and his men intended to grab Spanish New Mexico on their way to the "South Sea" (the Pacific Ocean). They believed that the United States intended to seize the entire continent. Orders were issued to arrest the explorers and stop the expedition.[1]

Luckily, the Spaniards didn't take immediate action. The American expedition spent five peaceful months—from December 1803 to mid-May 1804—at Camp Wood.[2]

Clark was in charge of the men, while Lewis was busy buying provisions and gathering information. The two leaders picked volunteers. Their party grew from the ten or twelve originally proposed to more than forty. Most recruits were enlisted army men who had received permission to volunteer. Since they continued to receive army pay, additional moneys weren't needed to retain them.

In addition to trained soldiers, Lewis and Clark hired French-Canadian rivermen who had experience navigating the waters of the Missouri. They engaged the most valuable man of their entire party, George Drouillard. He was a superb scout, an expert hunter, and a skilled interpreter who spoke several Indian languages and could "talk" using sign language. (His name was pronounced the way Clark spelled it in his journals, "Drewyer.")

During that winter, Lewis received upsetting news. The War Department had refused his request to make Clark a captain. (Clark was ranked by the army as a second lieutenant.) An incensed and indignant Lewis assured his friend that the men on the expedition would never know anything about his official rank in the army. They would address Clark as "Captain" and obey him as a co-commander.

Lewis and Clark visited St. Louis often and stayed with the Chouteaus, who were the richest fur traders in town. The Chouteaus briefed the captains about Indians, furnished journals and maps of the upper Missouri, and hired river pilots for them.

Indians welcomed goods offered by traders.

A chief of the Osages, a tribe well known to St. Louis traders

Many other people living in St. Louis proved helpful. A French physician supplied them with sulfur-tipped friction matches (not commonly used until twenty years later). The matches' instant fire would serve as a magic trick to amaze Indians.

A trader named John Hay taught Clark how to pack goods and gifts. Under Hay's supervision, seven bales were filled with blankets, clothing, tools, and other necessities, and fourteen bales with gifts for Indians. Each was marked to indicate whether the contents were intended for a head chief, a minor chief, or women and children. There were also medals, flags, and certificates that had been issued by the government.

The practice of giving medals to Indian leaders originated with the earliest explorers. The United States started issuing "peace medals" in 1789, the year George Washington became president. These were embossed with the clasped hands of friendship on one side, and the likeness of the president on the other. Ribbons or chains were used to hang the medals around Indians' necks. These medals were so treasured that many were buried with their owners.

Flags also made impressive gifts because many Indians believed they had magical powers. Indians often displayed them until they became rags filled with holes. It's a wonder that certificates acknowledging a chief's importance were valued at all, since the Indians couldn't read English. However, certificates were prized as though they contained mystical formulas.

In March 1804, Lewis witnessed the formal transfer of the Louisiana Territory from France to the United States. The ceremony took place in the frontier village of St. Louis. It was truly a banner day for him, seeing the Stars and Stripes unfurl as a symbol of expanding America. Lewis could now play an open, active role as diplomat.

He promptly sent messages to the Sauk, Fox, and Sioux tribes informing them that the people of the United States were "their fathers and friends." And he requested Pierre Chouteau to organize and accompany a delegation of Osage Indians to Washington, D.C., where they would be entertained by the "Great Father," Thomas Jefferson.

Lewis also prepared two boxes of articles that Pierre Chouteau was to deliver to the White House. These contained maps, Indian vocabularies, tree cuttings, specimens of silver, crystal, and lead, a ball of hair taken from the stomach of a buffalo (Jefferson was interested in everything!), and a

Front and back of a Jefferson Peace and Friendship Medal

The United States peace medal worn by the Indian chief in the foreground was a treasured possession. Any Indian who accepted a medal was expected to be loyal to the United States. This pledge of loyalty was especially important when the British and Spanish were competing with the United States for tribal friendship. With the exception of John Adams, every president from George Washington (1789–1797) to Benjamin Harrison (1889–1893) issued peace medals with his likeness embossed on one side.

cage containing a living specimen of a reptile new to science—the horned lizard.

Lewis anticipated from Jefferson's documents that mammoths, giants, and llamas might inhabit the West. The President also owned specimens of minerals said to have been taken from a "Mountain of Salt" that was 180 miles long and 45 miles wide. The President was so certain a salt mountain existed that he told the Congress about it.

Many people were convinced that a lost tribe of Welsh was to be found in North America. According to a popular version of history, Prince Madoc of Wales, accompanied by shiploads of followers, had settled in the New World in the year 1169. Madoc supposedly had discovered America three centuries before Columbus. There was speculation that Lewis and Clark would find Madoc's fair-skinned descendants still in possession of Welsh royal treasure.

Sergeant John Ordway and Private Joseph Whitehouse believed the Prince Madoc account. Lewis was skeptical, but didn't reject the story as nonsense.[3]

Welsh people, mammoths, giants, llamas, and mountains of salt! What were the Indians like? Many European scholars predicted that feeble, subhuman savages barely survived in the New World's stinking, swampy, insect-ridden West. Sergeant Gass had been warned about "savages of gigantic stature, fierce, treacherous and cruel."[4] But most of the men anticipated truly glorious adventures. According to Private Whitehouse, they "Hoisted Sail and Set out in high Spirits for the western Expedition."[5]

Drawing of a preserved horned lizard. Lewis and Clark sent a live horned lizard to President Jefferson.

4·The Voyage Begins

On May 14, 1804, as crowds cheered, the expedition left its winter quarters at Camp Wood. Twenty-two oarsmen, aided by a canvas sail, moved their keelboat up the Missouri River. There were also two open rowboats called pirogues, one manned by six, the other by seven oarsmen. Two horses were led along the banks of the river by hunters on the lookout for game.

The "Corps of Discovery" consisted of nine men from Kentucky, fourteen soldiers, two French rivermen, an interpreter, and the slave, York. In addition, there was a separate unit of seven soldiers and nine rivermen who expected to leave the group after reaching Mandan Indian territory up north. They were accompanying the permanent party "in order to assist in carrying stores or repelling an attack [from hostile Indians]."[1]

After a two-day journey, the explorers docked at St. Charles, an old French village consisting of a hundred houses and one church. They stayed there five days to wait for Lewis, who had been detained in St. Louis making final arrangements for the Indian delegation to Washington. At St. Charles, the men took on more supplies, repacked cargo, and had a very good time.

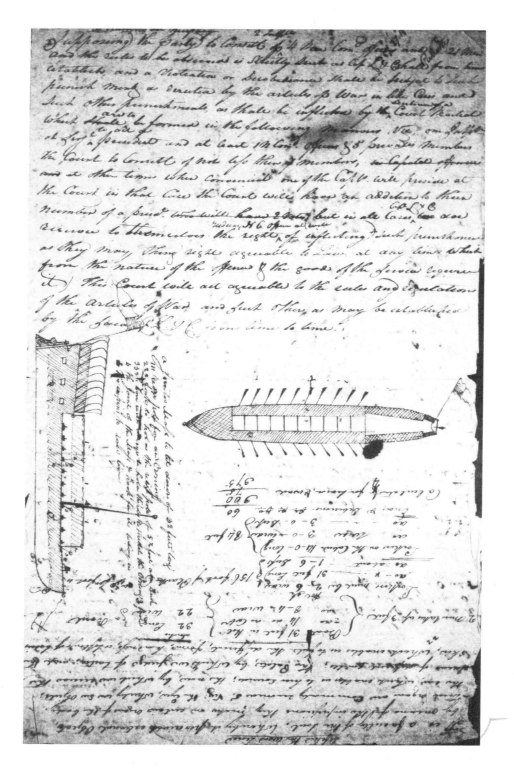

Clark's sketch of a keelboat

The stopover was fun—too much fun for three of the explorers who behaved "in an unbecoming manner" at a dance given by the villagers. A jury of soldiers handed down verdicts. The guilty soldiers were to be flogged (whipped): twenty-five lashes each for two men who stayed out all night; fifty lashes for a soldier who attended the dance without permission. (Flogging was commonly accepted as a means of disciplining military men.)

The day after Lewis arrived, the Corps sailed away from St. Charles, parties, and what they thought of as civilization.

Treacherous Waters

The waters of the Missouri River were challenging. The racing current meant hard rowing, and the sudden shallows required strenuous poling. The men often scrambled onto the banks or waded into the water, using ropes to pull their boats upstream. The banks frequently collapsed into the river, uprooting trees which then floated downstream. Mats of driftwood, sunken logs, and sandbars were a constant menace. The men spent hours up to their waists in swift, muddy waters, guiding the boats away from obstacles. Mosquitoes, gnats, and ticks pestered them. They suffered from sore feet, infections, and sunstroke.

Maintaining sound health was a problem. Lewis acted as physician. He gathered roots and herbs to medicate men for minor ailments. Dr. Rush's "thunderbolt pills" were usually prescribed for stomachaches. Lewis bled patients who had fevers or serious ailments. Fortunately, the men were hardy enough to recover from the weakening effects of bloodletting.

Most of the men, including Lewis and Clark, were ill at some time during their long journey. It is miraculous that only one man died. He was Sergeant Charles Floyd, diag-

Fur traders in a flatboat

nosed as having "bilious colic." Floyd probably died of appendicitis, a condition without cure at that time.[2]

However, there were days of smooth sailing, carefree travel, and fine camping. York gathered greens for wholesome salads from the river's bottom. Hunters supplemented the staples of salt pork and parched corn with deer, turkey, geese, and beaver. Roasted beaver tail was a gourmet treat. Hump of buffalo and haunch of deer were to prove equally delicious.

Lewis had brought along his pet Newfoundland dog, Seaman, who was both amusing and helpful.[3] Seaman acted

Lewis's dog, Seaman, was a Newfoundland, a large breed that typically weighs as much as 120 pounds.

as an expert hunter and sentinel. He caught squirrels and geese, and brought down deer that had been wounded by hunters. The dog was a strong swimmer, and could dive under water to force beavers out of their homes. He even managed to drown an antelope that had been swimming in the river. As a sentinel he was unique, for he could sniff out a bear or buffalo before any human was aware that an animal was nearby. Seaman was an asset for another reason. Indians viewed him as a curiosity. They had never seen a shaggy black dog. To them, Seaman looked like a tame miniature bear.

From time to time, the Corps passed trappers headed for St. Louis, their rafts and canoes filled with furs, buffalo grease, and tallow. Lewis was lucky to meet Pierre Dorion, a French-Canadian trapper who had lived among the Sioux Indians and spoke their language. Lewis hired him to join the group as an interpreter, and Dorion agreed to stay with them until they had journeyed past the dreaded Sioux tribes.

5·The First Powwow

TWO MONTHS WENT BY—and not an Indian in sight! The men had hoped to find native people when they reached the junction of the Platte and Missouri Rivers. Trappers had told them that Oto and Missouri tribes were there.

As soon as the boats reached the Platte, Lewis sent interpreters George Drouillard and Pierre Cruzatte to bring back Indians. They returned two days later. No Indians. They had found Indian villages, but they were deserted.

Five days later, while hunting, Drouillard came upon an Indian of the Missouri tribe who agreed to come back to the boats with him. The Indian spoke of a smallpox epidemic, which had killed most of the people in his village. Those who survived had moved in with their friends, the Otos. He explained that at this time of the year most of the Indians were away in the Plains hunting buffalo.

Using Drouillard as a sign-language interpreter, Lewis asked the Missouri tribesman to invite Oto and Missouri chiefs to a powwow. The man returned two days later with about a dozen men, six of them minor chiefs.

The Indians slept overnight in the expedition's camp. Because their contacts with white traders and trappers had always been peaceful, they probably enjoyed an untroubled

Oto chief

Missouri chief

rest. But Lewis and Clark's men were apprehensive. They feared that these people might attack, and they were on guard, "ready for any thing."[1]

The next morning a meeting was arranged on a bluff overlooking the river. Everyone sat under the shade of the keelboat's main sail, which was set up as an awning. Lewis delivered a speech that was to be repeated so many times that it became routine.

He addressed the Missouri tribesmen as "Children," and told them that "the great chief of the Seventeen great nations [states] of America" was "their only father . . . the only friend." His small audience was informed that American cities were "as numerous as the stars," and he invited chiefs to visit their "Great Father" Jefferson in Washington as guests (food, lodging, transportation, and all expenses would be paid). After warning his "red children" to "shut ears to

THE INCREDIBLE JOURNEY OF LEWIS & CLARK

The expedition's first council, as depicted by an engraver

the council of Bad birds [the English and French]," he promised that American traders would offer them better goods on better terms than they had ever received before.[2]

Lewis hung medals around the necks of the chiefs, and gave presents of leggings, garters, coats, blankets, gunpowder, and whiskey to everyone.

Gift packages were made up for Little Thief and Big Horse, important Missouri chieftains who had failed to show up for the powwow.

As a grand finale, a squad of soldiers paraded in full dress. Then Lewis created a sensation by firing off an air gun he had bought in Philadelphia. Using compressed air instead of powder, the gun shot quite accurately with popping noises, not loud bangs. Private Whitehouse described the Indians' amazement: "Soon as he had Shot a fiew times they all ran hastily to See the Ball holes in the tree as they Shouted aloud at the Site of the execution She would doe."[3]

After this sensational variety show, everyone left the meeting place. The captains named the site Council Bluff (located near present-day Fort Atkinson, Nebraska).

6·Excursions

THOUGH THEY NEVER WANDERED FAR from their boats, the men made interesting side trips. A visit to the grave of Omaha Chief Blackbird must have felt dramatic, although there wasn't very much to see.

Blackbird had died in a smallpox epidemic that had reduced his once-powerful tribe to about three hundred survivors. The chief had been known to hold up traders and grab some of their cargo before releasing them. He also poisoned members of his tribe who disagreed with him. According to reports, Blackbird was buried erect, astride his favorite horse. Lewis and Clark placed a white flag over the burial mound. This was a traditional Omaha way of paying respects to the dead. The explorers were probably told to do this by an interpreter or riverman who was familiar with Indian customs.

The magical "Mountain of Little People" was another side trip. This was said to be "the residence of Deavels that they are in human form with remarkable large heads, and about 18 Inches high . . . arm'd with Sharp arrows . . . Said to kill all persons who are So hardy as to attempt to approach the hill."[1] The men didn't find midget demons, only flocks of birds and bats that covered the dreaded "deavel's" hill.

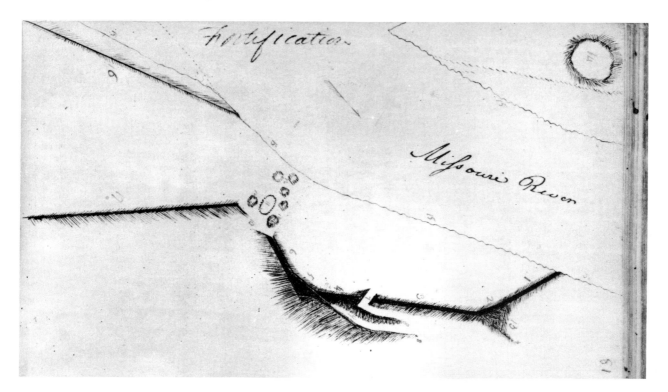

Clark's drawing of an Indian "fortification" on the Missouri River

Lewis often took excursions alone to collect plants and flowers. Many of those he found were new to him. Shortly after Council Bluff, he stopped to examine a beaver dam and marvel at its construction. He also climbed a cliff to test the soil. Lewis not only looked at it, but tasted it, "near poisoning himself by the fumes and taste." Clark reported that Lewis had to take medicine "to work off the effects of the arsenic."[2]

Clark was the expedition's mapmaker. He often walked along the riverbank in the evening trying to follow charts and maps that had been given to him. He also measured, described, and drew his own versions of land and water. At one point, the cliffs near the river seemed so uniformly shaped that Clark supposed they had been built as fortifications by ancient tribes. They were actually natural sand formations. But, despite his mistakes and although he was unschooled in the craft, Clark became one of America's finest mapmakers.

Excursions on land kept the entire Corps in high spirits. How fascinating it was to discover and examine animals never seen before! Private Joseph Field shot a badger, which was scrutinized as a great curiosity, then skinned, stuffed, and preserved for President Jefferson's collection. Lewis shot a white pelican. As an experiment, the men filled the mouth of the dead bird with five gallons of water. They were impressed with the capacity of the pouch.[3]

Prairie dogs were a new species that Lewis and Clark first

Prairie dogs, owls, snakes, and animal bones such as buffalo skulls were commonplace in the western wilderness.

saw in September. The men tried to dig them out of their burrows, but they couldn't catch any, even after they had shoveled six feet down. Then the men spent the better part of a day carrying water from the river in order to flood prairie dogs' tunnels. Success! One sopping wet "barking squirrel" came up for air and the men grabbed it.

Prairie-dog towns that stretched for miles were to become common sights. It was amusing to see thousands of heads pop out of holes, then disappear as soon as the creatures detected

Black-tailed prairie
dog, discovered
September 7, 1806

footsteps. Lewis referred to these rodents as barking squirrels because the animals burrowed and barked.

The men saw a "goat . . . verry actively made . . . his brains on the back of his head."[4] Clark shot one of them. The animals are commonly called antelopes; naturalists call them pronghorns. The goat with the brains on the back of his head was stuffed and preserved as a curiosity for that man in the White House.

On the same day they found their "goat," Private Shields killed a jackrabbit. This was a new species. When Lewis was able to observe a live jackrabbit, he marveled at its long, flexible ears, and estimated that its leaps measured from eighteen to twenty feet.

Prairie dog village

THE INCREDIBLE JOURNEY OF LEWIS & CLARK

Pronghorn antelope, discovered by the explorers September 14, 1805

As the Corps proceeded north, trees along the river became scarce and animals appeared in staggering numbers. Huge herds of buffalo covered the plains as far as the eye could see. Lewis was convinced that 20,000 buffalo would be no exaggerated estimate. As they moved deeper into the wilderness, vast herds of buffalo were everywhere. It became obvious that there were millions on the prairies and plains.

The men probably heard the baying and barking of coyotes before they saw them. Clark called the coyote a fox; later he changed the name to prairie wolf.

7 · Friendly Indians

Sioux Indian guard

THE EXPLORERS REACHED SIOUX TERRITORY in late August 1804.

The motion in sign language for Sioux is a throat-cutting gesture. The Sioux Indians earned their frightening reputation because certain Sioux tribes waged bloody battles against other Indians. Many white traders were so terrified of the Sioux that they would not proceed up the river for fear of confronting them.

President Jefferson had stressed the importance of winning the friendship of Sioux tribes. He had heard about their "immense power" as warriors, and wanted Lewis to "make a friendly impression" on them so that United States traders would be welcome in their territory.[1] Therefore, Lewis dispatched Sergeant Nathaniel Pryor and interpreter Pierre Dorion to find Sioux chiefs and invite them to a council.

When they reached a Yankton Sioux camp, Pryor and Dorion were relieved to receive a friendly welcome. The Indians offered to carry them to their chief on buffalo robes. Having lived with Indians, Dorion knew that only very important visitors were transported this way. He refused this honor, explaining that he and his companion were not leaders, and therefore would walk. Nevertheless, the Yanktons prepared a feast of "fat dog" in their honor, much to the delight of Sergeant Pryor, who remarked that the dog tasted "good and well flavored."[2] This hospitality was probably motivated by the Yanktons' need for trade and protection against attacks from the Teton Sioux tribe, which frequently raided Yankton camps.

Five chiefs and seventy warriors came back to the boats with Pryor and Dorion. According to Clark, the Indians were "Verry much deckerated with Paint Porcupine quils & feathers, large leagins and mockersons, all with buffalow roabs of Different Colours."[3]

Sioux chief and women with children. OVERLEAF: A Sioux camp. The women in the foreground are scraping buffalo skins to make them supple.

Everyone gathered under an oak tree (near present-day Gavins Point Dam, Nebraska). Clark named the site Calumet Bluff. *(Calumet* means *peace pipe*.)

Lewis delivered a long speech telling these "red children" that they must not fight other tribes, and that their "Great Father" in Washington would send supplies and gifts as a reward for their good behavior. Head Chief Shake Hand was then presented with a red lace-trimmed coat, a feathered cocked hat, an American flag, and a certificate of merit. All chiefs were given medals to hang around their necks.

When the meeting was over, Sioux boys staged an archery contest, and the explorers gave beads as prizes to the winners. At night, Indians with colorfully painted bodies sang and danced around the campfire to the rhythm of rattles and drums. According to Sergeant Ordway, their dancing "always began with a houp and hollow and ended with the same."[4] The crew rewarded performers with tobacco, knives, and bells.

The next morning, Chief Shake Hand made a point of telling Lewis and Clark that he already owned English and Spanish medals, and that another medal was meaningless and worthless. He preferred goods, because his people were very poor. Lewis explained that his men weren't traders and couldn't offer supplies, but that boats would soon come laden with the merchandise the chief's people needed.

After hearing this, Chief Shake Hand promised to make peace with other tribes, and agreed to send chiefs to Washington. Interpreter Dorion stayed behind to arrange a Yankton delegation to President Jefferson, while the Corps went on to confront another tribe of Sioux—the Tetons.[5]

8·A Troublesome Tribe

THE TETON SIOUX were known to stop boats and force traders to forfeit cargo as a toll. Sometimes they compelled rivermen to sell goods at ridiculously low prices, then profited by reselling the goods to other Indians.

The Tetons also sold British merchandise, which they acquired at annual intertribal fairs in South Dakota. Tribes along the Missouri River were their customers, and they didn't want white traders competing with them. That is probably why they tried to prevent boats from proceeding up the river.

The explorers were obligated to confront the Tetons even though they had been warned that the tribe was dangerous. Lewis was even supposed to arrange friendly councils—orders from President Jefferson, who had specified that he wanted all Sioux tribes as allies. However, before dealing with the Tetons, the Corps prepared against attack. Armed with rifles and swivel guns, they were alert to danger.

On the evening of September 23, three Teton boys swam up to the keelboat to greet the explorers. Their tribe lived nearby (opposite present-day Pierre, South Dakota). The captains asked the boys to tell their chiefs that white men wished to meet with them.

An island in the Bad River was selected as the site for a

The Scalp Dance featured enemies' scalps attached to poles.

An Indian council

council. The captains set up an awning, planted an American flag next to it, and unpacked gifts. Their rifles were loaded and the men "prepared all things for action in case of necessity."[1]

More than fifty Teton warriors arrived, headed by two rival chiefs: Black Buffalo, who was anxious for friendship, and Partisan, who was intent upon spoiling the powwow.

After eating and passing peace pipes, Lewis delivered his speech about the Great Father in Washington taking care of his red children.

THE INCREDIBLE JOURNEY OF LEWIS & CLARK

The Tetons couldn't understand a word. (It had been a mistake for the Corps to leave its qualified interpreter, Dorion, behind with the Yanktons.) French riverman Pierre Cruzatte, who acted as interpreter, knew only a smattering of the Teton language. As a result, Lewis's speech was boring gibberish to the warriors, and when an Indian's reply was relayed by Cruzatte, the captains could hardly understand what he was saying.

The conference perked up when the Corps's soldiers dressed in uniform and paraded in front of the Indians. Then Lewis ceremoniously handed out gifts. Chief Black Buffalo accepted a medal, a military coat, and a feathered hat. Lewis had made a diplomatic mistake. He didn't know that the tribe had two leaders who were rivals, and he had given Partisan lesser gifts.

Partisan responded to the insult by becoming obnoxious. When the Indians were given a tour of the keelboat, and were treated to shots of whiskey, Partisan pretended to be drunk. Although the gulp of liquor he consumed wasn't enough to affect his behavior, he reeled around the boat and jostled Clark. The explorers had a hard time getting Partisan and the other Indians into a pirogue in order to row them to shore.

As soon as the pirogue landed, three Tetons tried to hijack it by grabbing its cable. According to Clark, Partisan was "verry insolent both in words & justure . . . declareing I should not go on, Stateing he had not received presents sufficient from us."[2]

Clark drew his sword and warned the Tetons that he had "more medicine on board his boat than would kill twenty such nations in a day."[3] Black Buffalo immediately ordered the Indians to release the pirogue.

That night Black Buffalo and some of his followers were allowed to sleep on board. The crew was on guard all night, alert against attack.

Probably in an attempt to detain them, Chief Black Buffalo invited Lewis and Clark to his village. The next day the keelboat was anchored close to shore, and at night the captains and some of the crew disembarked to attend an Indian feast.

The menu featured barbecued buffalo, prairie parsnips, and platters of roast dog meat—a "delicious treat," according to Sergeant Ordway. The explorers were seated next to Black Buffalo. They faced a six-foot sacred circle that contained holy pipes and magic medicine bundles. (A medicine

Medicine bundle and its contents. Clark reported that large medicine bundles containing medals and other valuables were sacred. Only their owners dared touch them. Indians also wore small medicine bundles around their waists and necks as charms against evil.

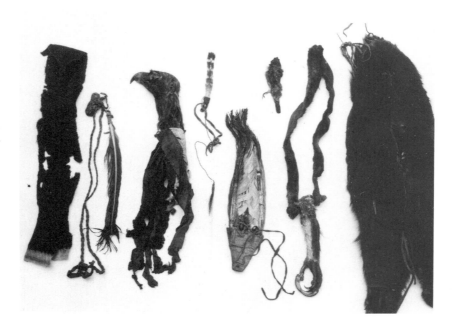

54

bundle might hold a buffalo skull, a perfect ear of corn, skins of birds, and bones of animals. Each bundle was different, and was believed by its owner to contain magical powers.)

Spanish and American flags were on display in the camp. These didn't signify Teton loyalty to Spain and the United States. To the Tetons, the flags were merely colorful decorations, not meaningful symbols.

The men watched a grisly performance of the Scalp Dance. About eighty women, holding sticks adorned with enemies' scalps, danced around a campfire. This was followed by male dancers who sang and pantomimed their brave exploits as fighters and hunters.

Dancing and singing continued until midnight. The party ended when Lewis and Clark politely asked to be excused because they were tired. Before they left, the Tetons offered to lend them women for the night. Much to the astonishment of the Indians, Lewis and Clark refused bedmates.

There was a repeat performance of the feast and dancing the following night. The next day, after four days with the Tetons, the captains decided to proceed upriver. Partisan, Black Buffalo's rival, again became a troublemaker. He ordered his men to seize the keelboat's cable, and refused to free the boat.

Lewis ordered all men to battle stations. Two hundred Indians armed with muskets, spears, and bows appeared on shore. Once again, Black Buffalo came to the rescue. He countermanded Partisan, and told the men to release the boat's cable. By doing this, Black Buffalo prevented a bloody battle.

Chief Black Buffalo was rewarded with a cruise up the river that was no fun when the waters got rough and the keelboat nearly keeled over. He was so frightened that he was happy to be put ashore.

9 · Refugees

As the explorers continued up the Missouri, they passed at least five abandoned Arikara villages. Smallpox epidemics had decimated a once-powerful tribe of Arikaras. Survivors of the disease had then become victims of attacking Teton Sioux.

At the time of the Lewis and Clark expedition, Arikara refugees had settled in three small villages, which had been fortified with ditches and ringed with walls. The villages were different from any the men had ever seen before. Instead of leather tepees or huts of bark, the Arikaras used round lodges made of willow branches, straw, and mud. These were thirty to forty feet in diameter—large enough to house several families and their horses.

The people were farmers whose crops included corn, beans, squash, and tobacco. They used buffalo shoulder blades for hoes, and deer antlers for rakes. The powerful Tetons forced them to sell at low prices whatever food they grew. The Arikaras had to allow their enemies to enjoy their crops. At times, when Arikaras tried to hunt buffalo, Tetons blocked their way to the herds. If the Arikaras wanted meat, they had to buy it from the Tetons.

The Corps reached the Arikaras during the second week

ABOVE: A bull buffalo

RIGHT: Arikara girl

THE INCREDIBLE JOURNEY OF LEWIS & CLARK

of October 1804. The captains met two men, Joseph Grave-lines and Pierre Antoine Tabeau, who lived and traded in the area, and who agreed to act as interpreters.

Lewis arranged the usual council. After the traditional smoke ceremony, he read a speech about United States power, the need for peace among tribes, and the benefits of protection and trade goods from Great Father.

After shooting the air gun and the keelboat's swivel guns to impress their audience, the explorers began the gift-giving game. They distributed medals and clothing to the chiefs, and red paint, mirrors, needles, razors, and tomahawks to the rest of the tribe. They also set up a corn mill, and showed the Indians how it worked.

Powwows often ended with swigs of whiskey. But, much to the surprise of Lewis and Clark, the Arikaras refused alcohol. They said that whites offered liquor in order to make Indians act like fools.

Magnets and phosphorous matches were effective magic to the Arikaras. But the hit of the day was York. The Arikaras had never seen a Black man before. After examining him and convincing themselves that he wasn't covered with

An engraver's depiction of trading on the Plains, where liquor was often offered in hope of taking advantage of the Indians. This Indian was shown looking doubtful.

York was admired by the Indians encountered by the expedition.
The Arikaras named him The Big Medicine.

dark paint, they expressed overwhelming admiration for this
big, strong, dark man. York enjoyed being the center of
attention, and in the spirit of fun, he clowned around, saying
that he was a wild people-eater. Clark was upset by York's
behavior. However, despite his feigned fierceness, York
charmed the Arikaras. They called him "The Big Medicine."
(The word *medicine* was adopted from English to mean
power.)

REFUGEES

One Arikara man was so intrigued with York that he invited him into his lodge to make love to his wife, then guarded the entrance so no one could disturb them. The husband was not just showing hospitality. He believed that close contact with The Big Medicine would result in some of York's powers rubbing off on his woman, and subsequently rubbing onto him.

Arikara women were enchanted with York. Although other members of the expedition enjoyed the favors of women, none was as popular as York.

The explorers enjoyed their five-day visit with the Arikaras. Clark described them as "durtey, kind, pore & extravigent." ("Extravigent" meant they were generous.)[1]

Lewis believed that he had convinced the Arikaras to reject the Teton business connection, but this was not so. Although the Tetons oppressed them, the Arikaras were reluctant to break away from their masters. They depended upon them for guns and other merchandise. Also, they dreaded reprisals from the Tetons, who were ever ready to raid their villages and strip their fields of corn.

The Corps's visit was not a total loss, however. The Arikara chiefs appointed a representative to accompany the expedition in order to meet and make peace with the Mandans, who were their enemies at that time.

On their way up the river, the Arikara representative was shocked when he witnessed a flogging. He cried aloud, declaring that his people never even whipped children. Hardened criminals were put to death, but not subjected to the cruelty of a beating. No explanation could change his disapproval of this brutality.

Liquor and flogging—were these important habits of the so-called civilized whites?

10·Winter Among Indians

By the last week of October 1804, icy patches and snow flurries made the captains realize that they had to stop for the winter and build a sturdy shelter. Lewis and Clark had heard many tales about Mandan Indians, who had been welcoming white traders ever since 1738. They decided to build a fort close to these friendly people (near present-day Bismarck, North Dakota).

The expedition spent the winter of 1804–1805 near two Mandan and three Hidatsa villages. These were situated on bluffs high above the river. Originally, the Mandans had lived farther south, but smallpox, then attacks by Sioux, had caused so many casualties that they moved next to the Hidatsas for help and protection. The Hidatsas tolerated the Mandans because they were good farmers.

Mandan and Hidatsa villages were the central market-places of the northern plains. French and English traders came there to barter guns and goods for furs. Cheyennes and Crows traveled from the West to exchange horses for food. Sioux Indians visited to barter buffalo meat for vegetables and tobacco.

However, many Teton and Arikara Indians didn't bother

Boats made of buffalo skin

OVERLEAF: Hidatsa village with earth-covered lodges

going to market. Instead, they raided Mandan fields whenever they wanted fresh food.

Sergeant Patrick Gass, who was an experienced carpenter, supervised the building of Fort Mandan, the Corps's winter quarters. There were log cabins, a large storage building, and a high picket fence for security.

Bitter cold and arctic gales made winter hard to bear. Hunting excursions were cut short because of the cold, and on at least one occasion the men didn't take the buffalo they

A winter buffalo hunt

shot, because they had to hurry home to the fort to warm themselves. One day, as an experiment, Lewis placed liquor outdoors. It turned to ice in fifteen minutes. One morning his thermometer registered fifty-four degrees below zero. Although the men would have enjoyed being outdoors, the intense cold forced them to stay inside much of the time.

Indians came to tour the fort and gawk at the odd-looking "tribe." They marveled at their strange clothes and equipment. Indians also came to sell their wares. A chief and his wife crossed the river in a buffalo-skin canoe in order to bring meat. After they landed, the woman carried the canoe on her back. The wife of Mandan Chief Big White also acted as porter. She carried one hundred pounds of meat on her shoulders. She was delighted when the explorers presented her with an axe. This was a gift any Mandan wife would have been thrilled to own, for a Mandan woman's work involved clearing fields and butchering animals.

Groups kept coming to admire the Newfoundland dog and York, the "unpainted man-with-the-black-skin." Sergeant John Ordway griped that the fort was overrun with Indians. He noted that one day fourteen Indians ate meals there, and he complained that the garrison was overcrowded and the Indians were "troublesome in our huts."[1] Private Joseph Whitehouse became so upset during one of their meals that he whacked the knuckles of an Indian whose table manners annoyed him. He was lucky the man didn't hit him back.

Indians brought women who stayed overnight. No one objected to that! Sometimes riverman Pierre Cruzatte livened things up by playing his fiddle, while the Corps danced jigs and square dances. These entertainments probably seemed as odd to the Indians as the "houping and hollowing" tribal dances had seemed to Sergeant Ordway.

Private John Shields became another popular attraction. He was the expedition's blacksmith, and the Indians enjoyed watching him work forge and bellows. They wanted him to make arrowheads and axes for them. Because the Corps needed a constant supply of food, Lewis and Clark permitted Shields to manufacture huge quantities of arrowheads and battle axes, in exchange for corn. They were arming Indians with war weapons at the same time they were trying to convince them to live in peace.

Several white traders lived among the Indians. Lewis hired a French Canadian named René Jusseaume to serve as adviser and interpreter. Jusseaume had lived among the Mandans for fifteen years. He moved into the fort with his Mandan wife and two children. Although the captains were irritated by his insolence, they were glad he was around. He spoke the Mandan language, knew tribal customs, and could list the names of Indian chiefs.

Another resident trader named Toussaint Charbonneau was also hired. He had been living in a Hidatsa village for five years, and, therefore, qualified as an interpreter. Charbonneau agreed to travel with the expedition on the condition that one of his wives could go with him. She was Sacagawea (sometimes referred to as "Bird Woman"). Sacagawea was a Shoshoni who had been captured from her tribe by the Hidatsas when she was a child—possibly when she was no more than twelve or thirteen years old. This little girl had been traded from man to man until Charbonneau acquired her. When Lewis and Clark met Sacagawea, she was sixteen or seventeen years old.

The captains were especially pleased that a woman who spoke Shoshoni would be with them. She would be invaluable when the explorers encountered her tribe. Only she could communicate with her people and convince them of the expedition's desperate need to buy horses.[2]

The Corps acquired not only a woman, but also an infant. Sacagawea's baby boy was born in a Fort Mandan cabin. Interpreter Jusseaume acted as attending physician. To hasten the birth, he prescribed two rings from a rattlesnake crushed and mixed with water. Fortunately, Lewis kept rattlesnake rings as antidotes against snakebite, and could supply them. After the strange potion was swallowed, Sacagawea gave birth in less than ten minutes. Lewis was skeptical about the effectiveness of the medicine, but he took notes. (His observations would surely be of interest to Dr. Rush.)

Visiting Indian Villages

The Mandans and Hidatsas welcomed the explorers into their homes. They lived in large, circular earth lodges, spacious enough to house several families and their horses.

Inside a Mandan lodge

Inside, dirt floors were honeycombed with deep storage pits that were filled with shelled corn and other harvested crops. Weapons, headdresses, enemies' scalps, and medicine bundles hung from poles.

Although several Hidatsa chiefs were not friendly, most Indian leaders were gracious hosts. Sergeant Ordway recalled that they were so cordial "they gave us different kinds of victules & made us eat in every lodge that we went in."[3]

Mandan Chief Big White became a close friend. He frequently invited the captains to his home, where he scratched maps on the dirt floor for their benefit. He also arranged for them to join buffalo hunts.

Lewis was particularly impressed with the integrity and intelligence of Mandan Chief Black Cat. The captain was under the impression that Black Cat was the villages' most powerful leader. Unfortunately, despite all the briefings about big chiefs and lesser chiefs, Lewis persisted in believing that one head chief was the decision maker. He and Clark never understood that one Indian tribe often had many chiefs of equal importance, and that chiefs' powers were usually limited. The Mandans, for example, were governed by a council of elders. However, the council didn't have absolute authority. It acted as an advisory board to all the people. Tribespeople usually accepted the council's opinions, but were not obligated to obey.

Indian Ceremonies

Winter among the Mandans enabled Lewis and Clark to watch many unique ceremonies. Their journals provided the first written descriptions of various Indian rites.

They witnessed Adoption Rituals. Enemies were adopted as "children" so that they could enter villages and trade in peace. As soon as they left, they were enemies again and

THE INCREDIBLE JOURNEY OF LEWIS & CLARK

subject to attacks. The Assiniboins from the north, for example, visited the villages while the explorers were there. As "children," the Assiniboins were tolerated by the Mandans until the tribes concluded their marketing. Prisoners of war also underwent adoption ceremonies, but they were accepted as permanent members of the tribe.

Feeding the Skull was another routine ritual observed by the explorers. After enjoying a hearty meal at one of the lodges, Sergeant Gass was aghast when he watched a family ceremoniously present a bowl of food to a buffalo skull, saying to the skull, "Eat that."[4] By feeding skulls, Mandans were symbolically appeasing the spirits of killed buffalo.

A public Buffalo-Calling Ceremony was as fascinating as it was shocking to the explorers. During this observance, young men offered their wives to old men. The wives' bodies were believed to absorb the elders' buffalo-hunting abilities, which they could then pass on to their husbands. The explorers were invited to participate because it was thought that they had special powers worth absorbing. Sergeant Gass coyly stated, "Though we could furnish a sufficient number of stories and anecdotes, we do not think it prudent to swell our journals with them."[5]

The Buffalo Dance was a dramatic ceremony. Warriors wore the heads and skins of buffalo and performed a stomping dance. The display was another tribute to the animals the Mandans needed for survival. Buffalo furnished not only meat, but hides used for making boats and clothes, sinews that made fine ropes, and bones that were carved into tools and farm implements.[6]

White Man's "Medicine Days"

Although curious about their visitors' ceremonies, Mandans stayed away from the fort during "Great Medicine Day"

OVERLEAF: Buffalo Dance of the Mandan Indians, about which Clark wrote in his journal (January 5, 1805), "all this to cause the buffalow to Come near So they may Kill them."

(Christmas). Sergeant Ordway wrote that "the Savages did not Trouble us as we had requested them not to come."[7] Perhaps the Mandans assumed that secret rituals took place that were too sacred or too shocking to see, or perhaps they simply stayed away because they had been asked to.

On December 25, 1804, the men relaxed, ate, drank, and danced to the tunes of Cruzatte's fiddle. They fired off rounds of ammunition, and enjoyed "a merry christmas dureing the day & evening until nine oClok—all peace and quietness."[8]

New Year's Day, however, was celebrated among the Indians. Sixteen members of the expedition danced in the central plaza of one of the villages. Clark ordered York to dance, and noted that it "amused the Croud Verry much, and Somewhat astonished them, that So large a man should be active."[9] A French riverman stole the show. He danced on his hands!

The Indians were so delighted with the dancing that they rewarded the men with corn and buffalo robes. On New Year's night, a few revelers felt safe enough to sleep overnight in the Indians' lodges.

Although Lewis and Clark were pleased with the friendly reception of the Mandans, they had reason to be concerned about the Hidatsas' attitude toward them. The Hidatsas suspected Lewis's intentions and resented his telling them whom to trade with and whom to revere as Great Father. Some Hidatsas showed their hostility by refusing gifts and shunning medals as "bad medicine." They had satisfactory trade agreements with the British, and saw no reason to change their business connections.

As for promising peace, it seemed senseless. If they stopped raiding enemies, how would young men prove their valor? How would they avenge the deaths of relatives who had been killed by enemies? Through daring battle deeds, men gained status among their people. Success in war brought

Hidatsa warrior in the costume of the Dog Dance

THE INCREDIBLE JOURNEY OF LEWIS & CLARK

honor and respect, and could elevate a man to a position of chief.

The Hidatsas were so intent on fighting that in March, while the Corps of Discovery was still at Fort Mandan, warriors left to fight the Shoshonis—and *they were armed with arrowheads and axes that had been made by John Shields!* As a host, Lewis was a success, but as a diplomat he failed to influence the Hidatsas.

Despite this failure, Lewis and Clark's contacts with the Hidatsas proved vital to the success of their expedition. The Hidatsas knew their way to the Rocky Mountains, because they traded, raided, and stole horses from western tribes. By drawing maps in dirt and on buffalo skins, the Hidatsas gave the captains geography lessons that would guide them through a confusing wilderness. The Hidatsas stressed the importance of horses for mountain travel, and told the explorers to buy them from the Shoshonis. They knew that tribe well—they had captured Sacagawea from them.

Jefferson's "Medicine Bundle"

On April 7, 1805, the keelboat was sent back to St. Louis. Corporal Warfington was in charge, with six soldiers and three rivermen. On the way, he picked up at least forty-five Indians who wanted to meet Great Father and enjoy a grand tour of Eastern cities. It was disappointing to Lewis that no Mandan or Hidatsa chiefs would risk the voyage.

The keelboat carried nine boxes with items for Jefferson. Cages contained six live animals: four magpies, one prairie dog, and a sharp-tailed grouse. Boxes were filled with skins, skeletons, horns, and antlers of animals, many new to science. Some boxes held sixty-seven specimens of "earths, salts, and minerals." Others had sixty specimens of plants (including a root said to cure bites from mad dogs). There was also a

THE INCREDIBLE JOURNEY OF LEWIS & CLARK

This specimen of bearberry was among the shipment to Jefferson that left Fort Mandan April 7, 1805.

tin with "insects, mice etc.," which was certain to enchant the Great Father.[10] Buffalo robes, bows and arrows, a dictionary of the Mandan language, Clark's map of the Missouri River, and Clark's huge chart describing fifty Indian tribes were also packed.

The odd assortment of objects made an ideal "medicine bundle" for Jefferson. Its mysteries excited and inspired new visions for the President, and for scientists everywhere.

11·Journey into the Unknown

THE EXPLORERS LEFT MANDAN TERRITORY on the same day the keelboat left for St. Louis, April 7, 1805. Lewis and Clark continued up the river, using two pirogues and six new canoes that the men had constructed during the winter. The Corps consisted of thirty-one people, plus Sacagawea and her two-month-old baby boy, Jean Baptiste, nicknamed Pomp.[1]

This was the start of the journey into the unknown. According to Lewis, they were "about to penetrate a country at least two thousand miles in width, on which the foot of civilized man had never trodden." Everyone was exhilarated. Lewis wrote that the moment of departure was "among the most happy in my life," and noted that there was "not a whisper or murmur of discontent [from the men] . . . all act in unison and with the most perfect harmony."[2]

The Hidatsas had furnished reliable information about pathways to the Rockies. However, their instructions were hard to understand, because they described foot and horse trails, not river routes. Distances were measured in terms of travel time, not in miles. Yet Clark was able to change "many sleeps" into miles, and draw workable maps that led the expedition in the right direction.

Knowing which way to go was, of course, the prime

These warriors were painted only a few years after Lewis and
Clark passed by Assiniboin territory.

concern, but avoiding hostile Indians was another major worry. The captains had been warned that Assiniboin warriors hunted along the banks of the Missouri. According to Lewis, these Indians were "a vicious, illy disposed nation," and he feared that confronting them could mean catastrophe.[3] There was plenty of evidence that these tribesmen were near. The men saw their tents and steam baths, and noticed red prayer cloths draped over tree branches. Fortunately, the group never encountered the Assiniboins, who were probably too busy hunting to bother about a stray strange group of travelers.

The river was the expedition's worst enemy. Tow ropes were needed almost daily because of shifting sandbars, falling banks, strong currents, and risky rapids. Men spent hours in bitter cold pulling and guiding boats. Sometimes they scrambled ashore, where cactus barbs stabbed their feet as they tugged at tow lines. Sand carried by strong winds inflamed

Many tribes used steam baths for health purposes. After spending time in the hot steam, plunging into the river, even in freezing weather, was common practice.

their eyes, and they were constantly cold. Even in May, snow fell and ice froze on their oars.

But at least no one went hungry. Game was plentiful, and the animals were so tame that deer, elk, beaver, and buffalo could be clubbed or shot at close range. The land was so crowded with animals that at times the men had to push buffalo cows and calves out of their way.

There was one "verry large and turrible animal" that was dangerous to hunt: *Ursus horribilis,* the grizzly bear.[4] Even when badly wounded, the animal charged its attackers. Private John Colter had to throw himself into the river to escape its claws. Private Hugh McNeal was treed by a bear one day, and couldn't climb down until the grizzly left at night. Despite the danger, the men wanted to cook with bear grease and eat bear steaks. But they hunted cautiously, the way the Indians did—in groups.

Sacagawea was expert at supplying food. She knew just

The Indian way of attacking grizzly bears was a cooperative group effort.

where to dig for tasty roots, and found nests where rodents hoarded vegetation. This remarkable young woman proved to be an intelligent, lovable, and useful addition to the expedition.

What a contrast to Charbonneau, who owned her! He was a temperamental, unstable character. Lewis described him as "a man of no peculiar merit."[5] Charbonneau was so inept as a riverman that he nearly wrecked the pirogue, along with its precious cargo of journals, medicines, weapons, and specimens. At the helm when a sudden squall caused the boat to keel over on its side and fill with water, he panicked, dropped the tiller, and prayed to Heaven for help. His life and the lives of several others (including Sacagawea and Pomp) were in danger because they didn't know how to swim.

His hysterics stopped only when riverman Cruzatte threatened to shoot him if he didn't grab the helm. Charbonneau righted the craft, while two men bailed out water. Sacagawea, with her baby strapped to her back, scooped up most of the light articles that had been washed overboard, and saved almost everything that floated.

As a pilot Charbonneau was a disaster, but he had one redeeming feature: he proved to be a creative French chef. The men praised the flavor of a unique sausage made of buffalo guts, dipped in the river, boiled, then fried in bear grease. The men proclaimed that this dish was "one of the greatest delacies [delicacies] of the forrest."[6]

On May 26, 1805, Lewis saw the distant Rocky Mountains for the first time. He was elated at the thought of being so near the source of the Missouri River, but he was also apprehensive. He realized that snow-covered mountains were barriers to the Pacific Ocean, and that suffering and hardship lay ahead.

The men of the Corps were used to seeing thousands of buffalo, but they were astounded when they came upon at

Indians often hunted buffalo by stampeding them over a cliff.

least a hundred rotting buffalo carcasses below a cliff. Indian hunters frequently killed buffalo herds by forcing them to stampede over a precipice. One Indian acting as a decoy covered his body with buffalo skin and wore a cap resembling a buffalo head. The decoy raced in front of a herd and headed for a cliff, while other Indians chased the herd from the rear, until the animals fell to their death. The Indian decoy jumped aside at the brink. If he wasn't quick enough he went over the cliff, too.

Turning Point

Clark had no trouble charting the expedition's course until the Corps came to a fork in the river that none of their Indian advisers had mentioned (near present-day Loma, Montana). Two months of traveling time had already passed. It was June. If the men went up the wrong branch of the river, they might be trapped in the wilderness. A correct

decision was critical. They had to follow the Missouri River
to its source.

Which branch should they take? The crew favored the
north fork because its muddy waters matched the color of
the Missouri. However, after surveying both branches, the
captains chose the south fork just because it wasn't muddy.
They concluded that its crystal clear water and its rocky bed
indicated that the stream flowed down from the mountains.

The Milk River, seen by the expedition May 9, 1805

Lewis and Clark were convinced that the south fork would take them to the Rockies.

Before setting out, they lightened their loads by burying equipment. The men made Indian-style caches. They dug holes and lined them with dry sticks, then filled them with tools, specimens, ammunition, and rations. They covered the contents with leather, which they then topped with sod.

On June 11, Lewis went ahead on land with a party of four, and Clark and the others proceeded by boat. Lewis knew that Clark and his men were not going up the wrong creek when he arrived at the Great Falls, for the Hidatsas had said he would see beautiful cascades.

The Great Falls

Lewis was overwhelmed by the beauty of "this majestically grand scenery,"[7] and declared it was the grandest sight he had ever beheld.

When Clark's party joined Lewis, the Corps set up camp. Many, including Sacagawea, were seriously ill. Time was needed to doctor the sick and to prepare for an overland trek around the Falls. The party would have to carry boats and gear over rough ground for more than eighteen miles.

The men built crude wagons to carry canoes and supplies. Their pirogue was hauled out of the water and hidden in the bushes.

Portage around the Falls was agonizing. The men struggled over jagged rocks and steep slopes. They endured oppressive heat and sudden cloudbursts. One day, hailstones as big as eggs bruised their bodies. Mosquitoes pestered them, and rattlesnakes were frequently under foot. Fear of grizzlies caused each man to sleep with a weapon at his side.

When they were ready to set their canoes in the water

The Great Falls of the Missouri River

again, Lewis hoped his collapsible iron boat would prove useful. After it was assembled, the *Experiment* floated like a cork, but then it leaked and had to be abandoned.

The explorers hoped their ordeal would end when they reached the Shoshonis and could buy horses.

12·Finding Shoshonis

Captain Lewis called this spectacular canyon "the gates of the rocky mountains" in his journal, July 18, 1805.

AFTER THEIR HARROWING TREK AROUND THE GREAT FALLS, the men paddled, poled, and pulled their boats toward the mountains. The second day out they saw fresh horse tracks and passed a large abandoned Shoshoni camp. The captains searched inland, sighted smoke signals, and followed trails, but saw no one.

When the boats reached three forks in the river, Sacagawea exclaimed that she had been kidnapped from her tribe at this place. They were in Shoshoni territory. The captains decided to set up camp and rest there. Clark and many others were sick and painfully lame. Prickly pear thorns had slashed their legs and punctured their feet. After several days' rest, when they felt able to continue, they followed the middle branch of the three forks, which they named the Jefferson River.[1]

Though Clark usually acted as chief scout, he was too lame to explore. Therefore, Lewis and three other men went inland looking for Indians. After two days of wandering, Lewis spotted a Shoshoni on an "eligant" horse. Overjoyed at the prospect of greeting him, Lewis walked slowly toward the mounted man. He held up trinkets as a lure. However,

THE INCREDIBLE JOURNEY OF LEWIS & CLARK

instead of riding to him, the Indian brought his horse to a halt.

Lewis also stopped. He waved a blanket in the air three times. (This was a sign of peace that he may have learned from Sacagawea.) Then he shouted "ta-ba-bone," a Shoshoni word that he thought meant *white man*. Unfortunately, the word meant *stranger*. (The Shoshonis had never seen a white man; therefore, there was no word for one in their vocabulary.) The Shoshoni galloped away from the self-proclaimed "stranger." All strangers were viewed as potential enemies.

On August 12, the day after this disheartening incident, Lewis's group crossed the Continental Divide—the ridge of the Rocky Mountains that separates the eastward flowing streams from the westward flowing waters. They celebrated with a drink from the stream that Lewis assumed to be the source of the Columbia River, which he thought would take them to the Pacific Ocean. (The stream was not part of the Columbia; it was part of the Lemhi River.)

However, the excitement of the day couldn't erase Lewis's gnawing fear that without horses his expedition would fail. He had to find Shoshoni horse traders and buy packhorses to carry their supplies across the mountains.

The next day he came upon three Shoshoni women. One ran away, but two stayed, possibly paralyzed with fear. They lowered their heads as if they expected to be killed. Lewis walked over to them, handed them trinkets, and daubed their cheeks with red paint. (Sacagawea had taught him that this was a gesture of peace.) The women agreed to lead them to their camp.

On the way, Lewis and his companions were startled by the approach of sixty mounted warriors, armed for battle. Lewis was clever and brave enough to lay down his gun. Carrying a flag, he walked toward the warriors. Meanwhile, the women showed off their gifts and indicated that the strangers were friendly. A chief dismounted and embraced

A Shoshoni with ceremonial pipe

THE INCREDIBLE JOURNEY OF LEWIS & CLARK

the captain. Lewis was relieved to receive a friendly welcome—even though he didn't enjoy "the national hug" because he was "besmeared with their grease and paint."[2]

The Indians brought Lewis and his companions to their camp and escorted them to Chief Cameahwait's tepee, where they were seated on green boughs and antelope skins, ready for council. Drouillard, using sign language, acted as interpreter.

The chief talked about his people's poverty and their need for guns to hunt for food and to fight enemies. Lewis spoke about his urgent need for horses and guides, and explained that more men of his group would soon arrive. Clark's party was paddling up the Jefferson River to join him. Lewis asked Cameahwait to send men with horses for the newcomers.

When Cameahwait was told that more whites were coming, he became suspicious. Additional strangers with guns! The white men might be in league with his enemies, the Blackfeet. Perhaps they planned to attack his people. Chief Cameahwait refused to send men to meet Clark. He changed his mind only after Lewis challenged his bravery and asserted that "among whitemen it was considered disgraceful to lye or entrap an enimy by falsehood."[3] To allay Cameahwait's fears, Lewis and his group handed over their guns to him. By doing so, they made the chief feel safe.

Sacagawea Sees Her Tribe

Sacagawea

When Clark's boats arrived and Sacagawea disembarked, she began to dance and suck her fingers—a gesture in sign language that she had seen her own people. Clark was greeted with many greasy "national hugs," and shells were tied to his hair. Crowds of Shoshonis gawked at white-skinned men, and at dark-skinned York, for they had never seen people that looked like this before. It was such an exciting day for the Indians that they postponed the traditional opening day of their buffalo hunt. Chief Cameahwait and both captains decided to hold council. Drouillard's expertise at sign language was no longer vital because Sacagawea, who spoke Shoshoni, would act as interpreter. This was her most significant role.

As soon as she saw Chief Cameahwait, she jumped up, embraced the chief, threw her blanket over him, and wept. *He was her brother!* The chief seemed moved, "though not in the same degree."[4] Sacagawea tried to control her emotions while acting as interpreter, but she broke into tears from time to time.

During the discussion the captains learned that the Shoshonis were so poor they often went hungry, and that Hidatsa and Blackfeet Indians periodically attacked them, stole horses, and killed their people. Chief Cameahwait wanted guns. Because the Corps needed horses to carry baggage over the mountains, Clark promised that "whitemen would come to them with an abundance of guns and every other article necessary to their defence and comfort."[5]

Once again the explorers were arming Indians for warfare, though they were supposed to sponsor peace. Their guns might very well be used against the battleaxes they had supplied to the Hidatsas. However, the captains felt compelled to provide weapons in exchange for which the Shoshonis agreed to help them.

Horse trading took place. At first an old shirt and a knife were enough to exchange for one horse. But day after day the price went up, and by the time Clark bought a horse he had to give up his pistol, his knife, and one hundred rounds of ammunition. After spending seventeen days with the Shoshonis, the Corps managed to acquire twenty-nine horses. Most of the animals were in poor condition, with sore backs.

The chief warned the captains that the path across the

Lewis, wearing a Shoshoni cape, posed for this portrait when he
returned from the expedition.

mountains was treacherous, and that there was "a great distance to the great or stinking lake as they call the Ocean."[6] The chief told them that the Pierced-Nose Indians, who lived on the other side of the Rockies, nearly starved whenever they crossed the mountains. Nevertheless, Lewis decided that if Indians could cross over, his men could, too. A Shoshoni guide nicknamed Toby agreed to lead them.

Before leaving, Lewis sank his canoes in the river by filling them with stones to hold them down, and his men dug caches to hide excess equipment. Boats and gear were hidden so they could be retrieved by the Corps on their return trip across the continent.

13·Flatheads and Pierced Noses

ON AUGUST 30, 1805, the explorers started out on a trail so high and steep that horses kept falling and sliding down slopes. Rain, sleet, and hunger made life miserable. Five days after they started, it snowed and was so cold that their moccasins were frozen stiff. Their agony ended after they descended into a valley inhabited by friendly Flathead Indians (near present-day Sula, Montana).[1]

Clark noticed that the Flatheads were "light complected more so than common" and that they spoke in a "gugling kind of language spoken much thro the throat."[2] Some of the men compared the Indians' speech with the clucking of fowl or the noise of a parrot.

Light-skinned native people who spoke a strange language. Flatheads might be the lost Welsh tribe! Private Whitehouse was sure of it, and Lewis worked on a Flathead vocabulary list "in order that it may be found out whether they Sprang or origenated from the Welch or not."[3] He knew that scholars would want to analyze his notes.

During their three-day stay with the Flatheads, the explorers bought additional horses and swapped sick animals for sound ones. They ended up with forty large horses and three colts. Before tackling the mountains again, the men

camped at a place they named "Travelers' Rest," where they expected to stockpile meat. But their hunters failed to find game, and so they had to proceed to the mountains with meager rations.

The Ordeal

On September 11, 1805, the explorers took the Lolo Trail across "the most terrible mountains,"[4] the Bitterroots of the Rockies. They climbed along the ridges of slippery cliffs and inched around the rims of terrifying precipices. Snow fell, and the men shivered with cold. There was no game to hunt and nothing to eat.

In August 1805, the expedition met a friendly group of Indians at Ross's Hole, Montana. The sign-language name for these Indians is Flathead. They did not, however, practice head flattening.

Lewis brought out emergency rations, the portable instant soup he had brought from Philadelphia. It tasted so awful that the men killed and cooked one of the colts rather than subsist on the Captain's broth.

Clark was determined to find food. He and six hunters went ahead of Lewis and the others. At night they camped near a stream, which Clark called "Hungery Creek" because they had nothing to eat. The next day they killed and butchered a stray horse, cooked some, and hung the rest on a tree for Lewis's men—who at this point were eating candles, drinking portable soup, and sipping bear oil. The second day out, Clark and the hunters descended into a valley where they met the Pierced-Nose Indians. (They were near present-day Weippe Prairie, Idaho.)

A Nez Perce with shell
ornament in his nose

Pierced-Nose Indians

The French for "pierced nose" is *Nez Perce,* the term commonly used for this tribe. The tribe gained its name because some of its people inserted ornaments through holes in their noses.[5] Clark was relieved to be greeted with friendliness—and food. The Nez Perces served salmon, berries, and bread made from root-flour.

After gorging themselves, Clark and his men had upset stomachs. (Their illness may have been from overeating, from new kinds of food, or simply from weakness.) Two days after Clark's group arrived, Lewis and the main body of the Corps marched into the Nez Perce camp. After eating Nez Perce food, they too were sick. The Corps camped near the water, and when they regained their health, made five canoes the Indian way: they burned out logs instead of hollowing them with axes and chisels.

THE INCREDIBLE JOURNEY OF LEWIS & CLARK

A Nez Perce with ring in his nose

Clark visited one of the Nez Perce chiefs, Twisted Hair. In return for a Jefferson peace medal and trinkets, Twisted Hair drew maps on white elkskin. According to the Chief, it was only two sleeps to the Snake River, and five more to the Columbia River. The chief's maps turned out to be accurate.

Before leaving, Lewis rounded up his horses and branded them with a hot iron marked US CAPTAIN M. LEWIS. Chief Twisted Hair promised to keep the Corps's horses until the explorers returned. When the Indians were not around, the men buried their saddles and some ammunition in secret caches. On October 7, they launched their new boats into the Clearwater River. The Corps anticipated easy paddling. No more poling, pulling, and rowing against the current. They would be going downstream, and if Twisted Hair was right, they would soon be floating down the Columbia.

14·Rush to the Pacific

THE CURRENT WAS SO SWIFT that they traveled at breakneck speed. Even though the boats hit rocks, sprung leaks, and sometimes capsized, the explorers ran rapids one after another, unwilling to waste time by making overland detours. After watching some of the narrow escapes from disaster, their Shoshoni guide, Toby, deserted them.

The explorers stopped to buy food from Indians who were fishing and drying salmon on huge scaffolds. Although salmon was plentiful, most of the men preferred dog meat. According to Lewis, dog tasted better than venison or elk, and it was healthier. This disgusted many western Indians, who contemptuously called the explorers "dog eaters."

From the time the men reached the Snake River on October 10 until they reached the Columbia River on October 16, crowds of Indian sightseers gathered to see the aliens. When they reached the Columbia River, hundreds of Wanapam Indians greeted them with dancing and singing.

The Wanapams were the first head-flatteners the Corps had ever seen. Wanapam babies' heads were pressed between boards until the nose, forehead, and front of the skull were permanently flattened. Many West Coast tribes distorted heads for beauty's sake. Tattooed bodies, feet bound so they

Some Indians who lived west of the Rockies flattened the heads of infants to produce an elongated adult profile—a sign of beauty and high status.

THE INCREDIBLE JOURNEY OF LEWIS & CLARK

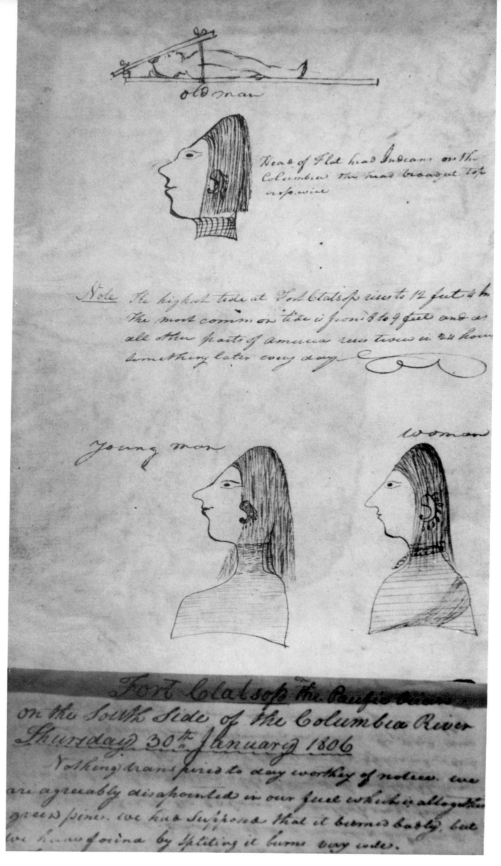

Clark's drawing of head-flattening process and its consequences

Fish was an essential part of the diet of Columbia River
people.

swelled, and shells through pierced noses were also commonplace. The explorers were shocked by these customs, and
considered them barbaric.

They were also baffled because the river's waters were
clogged with dead salmon. (Lewis and Clark didn't know
that adult salmon migrate from the ocean to rivers, where
they lay eggs and fertilize them, then die.)

One week after the expedition entered the Columbia
River, Celilo Falls blocked their way. It had a sheer

twenty-foot drop. An entire day was spent carrying canoes and gear overland. Then the men paddled down the river until they reached the treacherous Dalles Falls. Despite danger, they ran the rapids. They felt there was no time to lose. They had to reach the Pacific!

THE INCREDIBLE JOURNEY OF LEWIS & CLARK

Indians trapping salmon beneath waterfalls on the Columbia River

When the group saw Indians wearing sailors' jackets, they knew they were near the ocean. The clothes obviously came from British or Yankee ships that traded for furs along the coast. The Corps maneuvered its boats through another set of wild rapids, the Cascades. Then the expedition set up camp within sight of distant Mount Hood, Mount St. Helens, and Mount Washington.

Chinook Indians were constant visitors to their camp. They ate, smoked, received gifts, and enjoyed watching the explorers square-dance to the tunes of that strange instru-

ment, the fiddle. But playing host to Chinooks became unpleasant after Clark's pipe-tomahawk was stolen and a riverman's coat was pilfered. The captains decided that the Chinooks were an undesirable, thieving people. Nevertheless, they continued to see Chinooks, for good reasons. They

Mount St. Helens

were their source of food, firewood, and female company.

When the Corps reached the ocean in mid-November, elation was brief. The men became disheartened and depressed. They had crossed the continent, but fleas, bad food, thieving Indians, and wet weather dampened their spirits. After a four-thousand-mile trek across the continent, they had to endure a winter in an awful climate among people they disdained.

Fort Clatsop

Weeks were spent searching for a suitable campsite. The captains finally picked a location a few miles inland, beyond the sound of the sea, but supposedly situated near good hunting grounds. The captains named their winter quarters Fort Clatsop, after the local Clatsop Indians.[1] The camp's two rows of log cabins were small and cramped.

The winter of 1805–1806 was miserable. Only twelve days were free of rain, and six of these were overcast. The men spent most of their time indoors. Colds and fevers were common. Fleas tormented the men. They often stripped in futile attempts to rid their bodies of insects. It was so damp that clothing rotted and food spoiled. There was no liquor left and tobacco was rationed because the captains wanted to save it for trading purposes. Even Christmas dinner was a washout. Spoiled elk, spoiled fish, a few roots, and drinks of water were hardly their idea of a holiday meal.

Because salt would make their food more palatable, some of the men were sent to the ocean, where they spent days boiling seawater until their pots were coated with salt. The salt was then scraped into a barrel and carried to Fort Clatsop.

The men also managed to add whale blubber to their diet. When local Indians reported that a dead whale had been beached during a storm, Clark organized a sightseeing excursion. By the time his group arrived, the whale had been butchered by Indians, and only the skeleton was left. After measuring the 105-foot-long remains—another fact for Jefferson—Clark bought 300 pounds of blubber for the fort's food supply.

The men fought cabin fever by spending hundreds of hours making clothes to replace their mildewed, rotting wardrobes. They made shirts, trousers, and moccasins—338 pairs, more than they could ever need, but it kept them busy. Lewis and Clark worked on their journals. Clark drew maps of land and river routes from Fort Mandan to the coast. Lewis described hundreds of plants and animals new to science. He also wrote detailed accounts about Indian customs, costumes, and life-styles.

Clark's map showing the expedition's temporary encampment near the Pacific Ocean (lower right)

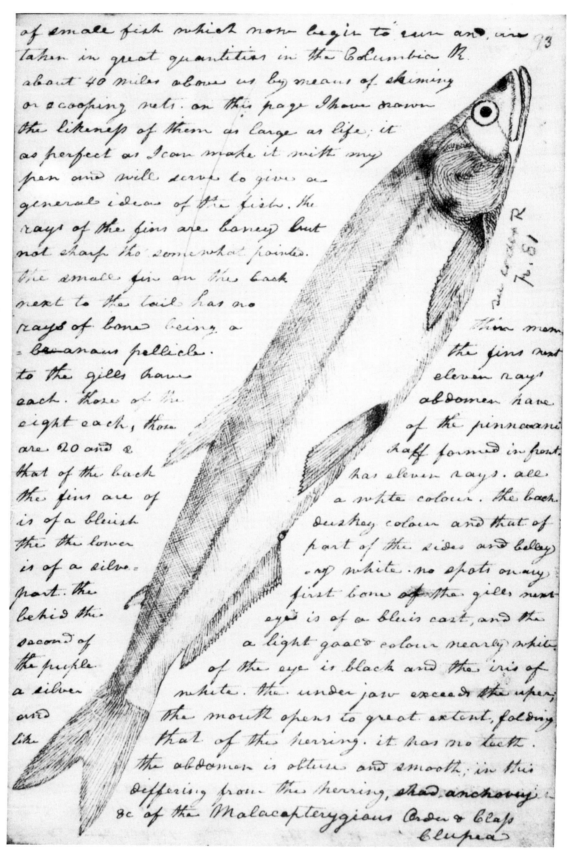

of small fish which now begin to run and are
taken in great quantities in the Columbia R
about 40 miles above us by means of skiming
or scooping nets. on this page I have drawn
the likeness of them as large as life; it
as perfect as I can make it with my
pen and will serve to give a
general idea of the fish. the
rays of the fins are boney but
not sharp tho' somewhat pointed.
the small fin on the back
next to the tail has no
rays of bone being a
= bononous pellicle.
to the gills have
each. those of the
eight each, those
are 20 and a
that of the back
the fins are of
is of a bluish
the the lower
is of a silve=
part. the
behind the
second of
the purple
a silver
and
like

thin mem
the fins next
eleven rays
abdomen have
of the pinnaani
haff formed in front
has eleven rays. all
a white colour. the back
duskey colour and that of
part of the sides and belly
ory white. no spots on any
first bone of the gills next
eye is of a bluis cast, and the
a light gaald colour nearly white
of the eye is black and the iris of
white. the under jaw exceeds the uper,
the mouth opens to great extent, folding
that of the herring. it has no teeth.
the abdomen is obtuse and smooth; in this
differing from the herring, shad, anchovey;
&c of the Malacapterygious Order & Class
Clupea

Clark's journal features this sketch of a candlefish.

The captains were in no mood to court the friendship of neighboring people who, they concluded, were dull-witted thieves. The Indians who visited the fort had to leave before sunset. The explorers couldn't talk to them, anyway. The Indians' language was a mystery to them, and coastal tribes didn't use sign language. Communication was limited to the few words that the men picked up.

The West Coast Indians were unhappy, also. They couldn't understand the attitude of their visitors. Why would white men travel such a great distance unless they wanted to buy furs? They were accustomed to sea captains who bought otter skins from them. Why were these poor sickly men huddled in huts in their territory? It is no wonder that they were suspicious, and they resented the Corps's unfriendly attitude.

President Jefferson had requested that at least two members of the expedition should return by ship carrying Lewis's notes with them. However, no one could see ocean traffic from Fort Clatsop. It is ironic that an American ship, the *Lydia,* spent the winter along the coast at the very time the explorers were boxed in at Fort Clatsop.

On March 23, 1806, the expedition left its winter quarters and headed back toward the United States, homeward bound.

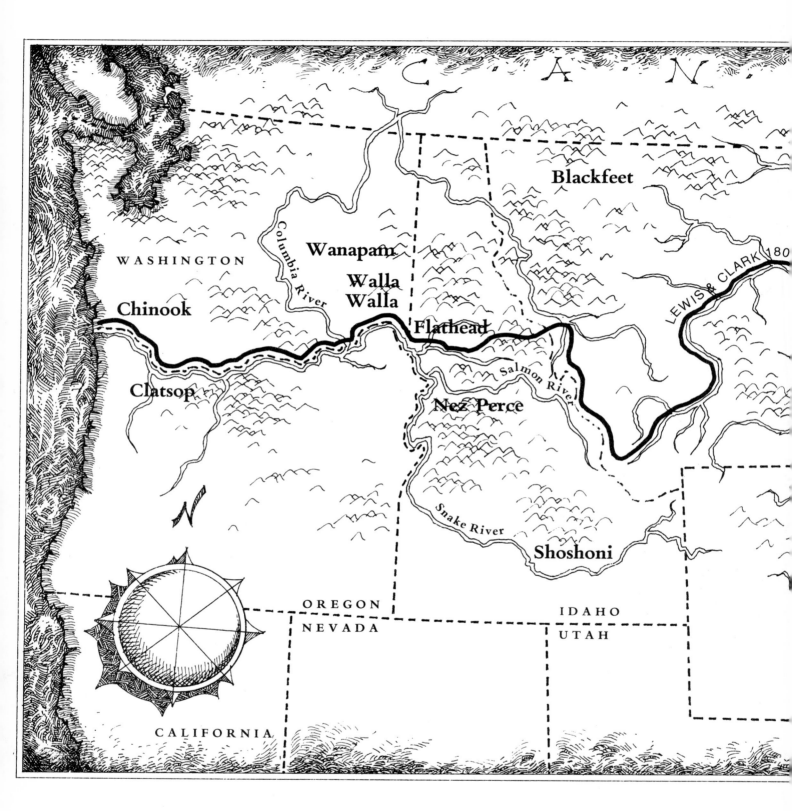

INDIAN TRIBES ENCOUNTERED

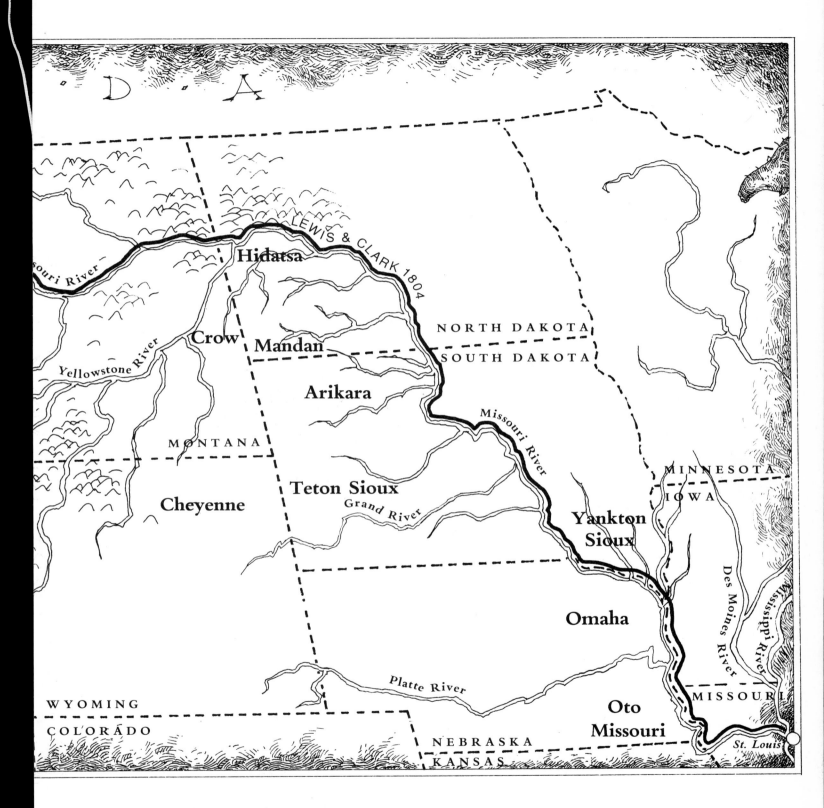

BY THE EXPEDITION

15·Homeward Bound

THE CAPTAINS FEARED that if they delayed leaving the West Coast, they would reach the Missouri when the river was frozen and they would be forced to endure another winter away from home. It would have been wise to wait until May, when salmon reappear in the rivers, because the fish would have guaranteed a food supply. But Lewis and Clark were impatient, and the men were eager to get going. (Since they didn't understand the life cycle of the salmon, they may not have known they would reappear.) In any case, they willingly settled for a diet of roots and dog meat.

Chinook Indians watched the explorers pull their canoes through the Cascade Rapids. Two of this "tribe of villains"[1] threw stones at them, and three others tried to kidnap Lewis's dog. But when the thieves saw armed white men chasing them, they let go of the dog, and ran away. Lewis was so furious, he warned the Chinooks that "if they made any further attempts to steal our property or insulted our men we should put them to instant death."[2]

Despite Lewis's rage and the anger of his men, who seemed "well disposed to kill a few of them,"[3] the Corps spent time with a Chinook chief named Coboway. Lewis

Lewis and Clark on the lower Columbia River. Sacagawea (right)
is gesturing to the Chinook Indians.

even managed to compile a list of Chinook words for Jefferson's vocabulary collection.

The explorers weren't among friendly natives until the end of April, when they reached the Walla Wallas. Their chief, Yelleppit, still cherished a peace medal the captains had given him six months before, when they passed through heading west. After greeting Lewis and Clark with a long-winded welcoming speech, Yelleppit ordered his people to supply them with fuel and food.

At Yelleppit's insistance, the Corps stayed for three days. During that time the explorers stocked up on food. Because they were short of gifts, Clark bartered his sword, and some of the men offered to exchange tin boxes, fishhooks, and odds-and-ends for dogs and other food. Clark also played doctor, accepting food as a fee for medicines. On April 30, the explorers left the Walla Wallas, "those honest friendly people,"[4] and headed for the land of the Nez Perce Indians.

Over the Mountains

News that the white explorers had returned to the Nez Perce area spread, and many people came to see the strange-looking white "tribe." Crowds inspired Lewis and Clark to arrange a powwow. Once again, the captains gave a speech that stressed the advantages of trading with the United States and the need for intertribal peace.

The explorers watched a unique Ritual of Acceptance. Indians who approved of the explorers' speech ate a thick mush that one of the chiefs had cooked and ladled into pots. While chiefs swallowed mush, women wept, perhaps because they felt that accepting white men's power was a tragic mistake.

The Corps set up Camp Chopunnish along the Clearwater

River near the Nez Perces. They spent nearly a month there—from May 14 to June 10. The Indians and explorers enjoyed one another's company. They danced, held races, and played games together. Many friendships developed. The men were particularly fascinated by one man who wore a cape made from the scalps and fingers of enemies he had killed. They presented this awesome warrior with a decoration for his costume—claws from a bear that Private Collins had shot.

Life wasn't easy at Camp Chopunnish, however. There was an acute food shortage. Once again, Clark set up a very active medical practice in exchange for dogs, which were willingly given. (The Nez Perces never ate dog meat.) He treated up to fifty Indians a day for everything from sore eyes to paralyzed feet. Luckily, many patients felt better. Clark was truly "good Medicine."[5]

Soldiers ripped buttons off their uniforms in exchange for something to eat. The captains supplied each man with "one awl and one knitting-pin, half an ounce of vermillion [red paint], two needles, a few skeins of thread, and about a yard of riband" so that each person could barter for provisions.[6]

The horses that had been left in Chief Twisted Hair's care were returned to the captains, and after having stocked up on food, Lewis and Clark felt ready for the most dangerous part of their journey: crossing the Rocky Mountains.

Even though the captains couldn't hire Indian guides, they dared to set out on June 15. Two days later they turned back. The snow was fifteen feet deep! This was the first time the captains were "compelled to retreat," and they were mortified.[7] On June·24 they set out again, this time with Nez Perce guides to lead them across the mountains. There were only a few inches of snow on the trail chosen by their guides, and the expedition was able to reach Travelers' Rest in six days.

Separate Ways

The captains decided to split up in order to explore new territory, then reunite at the Missouri River. Lewis was to follow the Marias River to its source. Clark was to explore the Yellowstone River.

Clark left Travelers' Rest on July 3 with twenty-two people (including Sacagawea and her child). His group did not see Indians, but Indians saw them. Horses were stolen while Clark's group was sleeping.

When Clark reached the Jefferson River, his men found the canoes that had been left behind. They also built new ones. Then Clark's party split up. Sergeant Ordway and ten men headed down the Missouri. Clark and the others trekked overland to the Yellowstone River, then paddled down the Yellowstone to the Missouri.

An Indian Fight

There were nine in Lewis's party. For the first few weeks, the journey was peaceful and the men only had to battle clouds of attacking mosquitoes. After ten days' travel, they reached the Great Falls, where they opened the caches they had dug the year before. Animal skins, plant specimens, and medicines had been spoiled by seeping water. Fortunately, Clark's map of the Missouri wasn't ruined, and they set it out in the sun to dry.

Five men were to go directly to the Missouri River, while Lewis, Drouillard, Reuben Field, and Joseph Field explored the Marias River. The captain hoped that the Marias River extended north into valuable, fur-rich territory, which could be claimed for the United States. (All land drained by tributaries of the Missouri was to be declared United States territory, according to the terms of the Louisiana Purchase.) After following the Marias for one week, Lewis was disappointed to find that the river flowed west, not north.

Lewis quickly decided to quit the area. He didn't want to meet up with Blackfeet Indians, who were known to frequent the region. A principal occupation of the Blackfeet was war. Shoshoni and Flathead tribes were among their many targeted victims. On July 25, 1806, Lewis wrote in his diary, "We consider ourselves extreemly fortunate in not having met with these people."[8] The next day, he saw "a very unpleasant site"—eight Blackfeet. He and his three companions were outnumbered two to one.

Lewis decided to act cordially. He permitted the Indians to camp with him. During a not-so-restful evening, Lewis

Blackfeet warrior

used Drouillard's sign language to tell the Blackfeet about the advantages of trading with the United States and living in peace with other tribes. His speech alarmed the Blackfeet. They were satisfied to trade with the Canadians, who supplied them with guns and liquor. They did not want to change their business connections. And they were certainly not going to stop raiding other tribes just because a white stranger told them to do so.

Lewis made his most serious blunder when he told them about his friendship with the Nez Perces and the Shoshonis. These tribes were enemies of the Blackfeet. It is possible that the Blackfeet suspected that Lewis had supplied their enemies with weapons.

Joseph Field was on guard duty that night. At dawn he became careless and laid down his gun. An Indian grabbed his gun and the gun of his brother, Reuben. Two other warriors took rifles belonging to Drouillard and Lewis.

Shouts from the Field brothers aroused the other men from sleep, and they gave chase. During the commotion, Reuben Field stabbed a Blackfeet in the heart. Then, when the Indians tried to run off with his horses, Lewis shot and killed another Blackfeet warrior. *This was the only time Indians were killed by members of the Lewis and Clark Expedition.*

The Blackfeet escaped so quickly that they left behind some of their horses and weapons. Lewis collected their abandoned shields and bows and arrows, but he was so angry he burned them instead of keeping them for Jefferson. (Lewis did keep the warriors' medicine bags and they ended up in a Philadelphia museum.) As a final act of fury, he placed a peace medal around the neck of one of the dead Indians so "they [the Blackfeet] might be informed who we were."[9] After the killings, Lewis and his group feared attacks from avenging Blackfeet. They did some hard, fast riding, and covered 120 miles in 24 hours.

What a relief to arrive at the Missouri River and see the

Blackfeet with guns that were probably obtained through trade with the British.

Corps's boats! Lewis and his three companions let their horses go and jumped into the canoes. After several days of paddling, they caught up with Clark's boats, which had gone ahead for good hunting and to escape pesty mosquitoes.

A day before the captains reunited, Lewis had been seriously hurt. While hunting for food, Cruzatte, who was stalking game with him, accidentally shot the captain in the buttocks. The riverman had mistaken the buckskin-dressed captain for an elk! Lewis gave full command to Clark. He didn't expect to recover from the painful gunshot wound for at least three weeks.

On August 14, 1806, the explorers were back with their friends the Mandans and Hidatsas. It had taken them four months and twenty-one days to travel from Fort Clatsop.

16·Back to Civilization

LEWIS AND CLARK HOPED that Mandan and Hidatsa chiefs would accompany them to Washington. Clark acted as spokesman, because Lewis was still ailing from his gunshot wound. He invited the chiefs "to visit their great father the president of the United States and to hear his own Councils and receive his gifts from his own hands."[1] The speech failed to lure volunteers. Going to Washington meant traveling past enemies, the Teton Sioux, and the chiefs refused to chance the trip.

Clark turned to René Jusseaume for help. Jusseaume found one chief willing to go. He was the captains' old friend, Big White. The chief could arrange to leave within twenty-four hours. However, Jusseaume wanted his own wife and two children to go with him, and Big White wanted to take his wife and child. Clark was annoyed by this group-travel plan, but because he wanted to bring home at least one Indian, he was "obliged to agree."[2]

Before leaving, the explorers settled accounts with Charbonneau, who decided that he, Sacagawea, and their child would resettle among the Mandans. The captains paid him $500.33 for his services on the expedition. No one would miss this inept, irritating man, but Sacagawea and her son

Big White, the Mandan chief who accompanied Lewis to
Washington, D.C.

Bighorn, discovered
April 26, 1806

had been a joy. Clark revealed his affection for the "butifull promising child" by offering to take him to St. Louis and "raise the child . . . in such a manner as I thought proper."[3] But the parents said that a nineteen-month-old baby was too young to leave them. (About five years later, Pomp was sent to live with Clark.)

When the explorers left after a three-day stay, many Indians were upset that Big White accompanied them. Some of them wept because Big White was daring to explore the mysterious lands of the East. They were certain they would never see him again.

Hoping to recruit at least one more chief to present to Jefferson, the captains stopped at an Arikara village. No success. The Arikaras had already sent one chief to Washington. He had been gone seventeen months and there had been no news from him. They refused to send another delegate until this chief returned.

Just a few days after the explorers' visit, a trader brought the Arikaras the tragic news that the chief who had gone to Washington had become ill and died. The trader delivered the dead man's clothes and gave the dead chief's son a peace medal, a certificate of honor, and a condolence note from Jefferson, which explained, "everything we could do to help him [the chief] was done; but it pleased the Great Spirit to take him from us . . . we shed many tears over his grave."[4] A medal and some papers they couldn't read offered no comfort to the Arikaras. They were appalled, and concluded that white men were enemies who should never be trusted. After that, they were hostile toward white men. (The explorers were lucky to have visited *before* the Arikaras found out about their chief.)

When the Corps passed Teton Sioux territory, a large band of warriors hooted and dared them to land. The explorers were wise enough to avoid them.

The captains did stop to smoke peace pipes with a group

Sage grouse, discovered
by Lewis June 5, 1805

THE INCREDIBLE JOURNEY OF LEWIS & CLARK

of Yankton Sioux. According to Clark, "one of them Spoke and Said that their nation had open their years [ears] & don as we directed ever since we gave the Meadel [medal] to their great Chief." Because of their attitude, the explorers "tied a piece of ribbon to each man's hair and gave them some corn."[5]

Despite the rush to return, Lewis and Clark took time out to find more scientific specimens. They added plants, a dead magpie, and "sceletons" of prairie dogs, a mule deer, and an antelope to their collection.

Blacktail, or Mule, deer, discovered September 17, 1804

Mountain quail, discovered April 7, 1806

Woodpecker, discovered April 7, 1806

Leaves of evergreen shrub, drawn by Clark April 10, 1806

As they traveled south, they met American traders who were astounded to see them. Most people had assumed that Lewis and Clark were dead. One man exclaimed that the entire expedition "had long Since given out [up] by the people of the U S Generaly and almost forgotten." But, he added, "The President of the U. States had yet hopes."[6] At least Jefferson remembered them.

Everyone at St. Charles was astonished when the Corps showed up on September 21. The expedition had been gone for such a long time that people assumed the men had met a tragic end. According to one rumor, wild Indians had slaughtered the entire Corps. According to another, Spaniards had captured the explorers, then forced them to work as slaves in Mexican mines.

The expedition arrived in St. Louis on September 23, 1806—two years, four months, and ten days after it had left. The men had journeyed more than seven thousand miles. Crowds lined the banks of the river to shout "harty welcome" to adventurers who had courageously dared to explore uncharted lands. Dressed in tattered buckskins, they looked like trappers who had spent their whole lives in the wilderness.

Their appearance changed as soon as they bought clothes at the public store. Even Chief Big White was induced to shed his Indian costume and dress like a "civilized" citizen.

Messengers spread the news about the miraculous appearance of the explorers. A letter from Lewis to Jefferson was sent up the Mississippi to the United States postal station at Cahokia, Illinois. Then a rider delivered it to a very worried President Jefferson. Lewis wrote that he was certain the expedition had "discovered the most practical route which does exist across the country," and that he and Clark "view[ed] this passage across the Continent as affording immence advantages to the fur trade." He noted that "the

Missouri and all its branches . . . abound more in beaver and common otter than any streams on earth."[7]

Jefferson reacted with "unspeakable joy."[8] In a message to Congress, he proudly announced that his explorers had "traced the Missouri nearly to its source, descended the Columbia to the Pacific Ocean . . . [and] learned the character of the country, of its commerce and its inhabitants."[9]

As a reward for their expedition, Congress voted double pay for each member of the Corps and awarded 320 acres of land to each enlisted man. Lewis and Clark each received 1,600 acres. Meriwether Lewis was made Governor of the Louisiana Territory. William Clark became Brigadier General of the Louisiana Territory Militia.

Buzzard's head,
sketched by Clark
February 16, 1806

Heroes of an Incredible Journey

Lewis and Clark put an end to fables and fantasies about the West. They had explored territory as mysterious to them as the Western Hemisphere had been to Columbus. North America, with its huge mountains and vast plains, proved to be much wider and more beautiful than geographers imagined. The men had not encountered monsters or mammoths. And instead of cruel, subhuman savages, they had met many friendly tribes who fed, advised, and guided them. Indeed, without the help of Indians, the expedition party might not have survived.

Lewis and Clark's accomplishments were astounding. They discovered and described 122 animals new to science. (These include the coyote, prairie dog, porcupine, polecat, jackrabbit, bull snake, tern, trumpeter swan, and steelhead salmon trout.) And they found 178 new types of plants. (These include trees, shrubs, grasses, flowers, fruits, and vegetables.)

Bitterroot, discovered July 1, 1805

Black-billed magpie, discovered September 16, 1804

The captains also brought back a vast body of information about Indian tribes of the West. There were vocabulary lists, estimates of tribal populations, and details about ceremonies, costumes, and customs. More than forty tribes were studied. The Shoshonis, Flatheads, Nez Perces, and Walla Wallas were among those whose life-styles were documented for the first time.

Although Lewis and Clark failed to find a water route across North America, they succeeded as great scientists and as heroic pathfinders who drew the nation west. Trappers, traders, travelers, and settlers followed their trails.

After their incredible journey, the United States could dream of becoming a nation whose lands reached the Pacific.

THE INCREDIBLE JOURNEY OF LEWIS & CLARK

Aftermath

Meriwether Lewis committed suicide three years after his return from the glorious expedition. He was only thirty-five years old. It is a pity that life became unbearable for this great scientist-explorer.

Although his appointment as Governor of the Louisiana Territory was an honor meant as a reward for his accomplishments, Lewis was miscast and miserable as an executive. He was not cut out to be an administrator, and his decisions were frequently criticized by other officials. Governor Lewis was particularly offended when his modest, legitimate expenses were questioned by members of the new administration of President James Madison.

Personal problems also plagued him. He was an unhappy bachelor whose marriage proposal (or proposals) had been rejected. After settling in St. Louis, he was short of money and feared bankruptcy, as a result of unwise real estate investments. He had hoped to bring his widowed mother to St. Louis and provide a home for her near him, but lack of funds made this impossible.

The publishing of his journal was another source of distress. Although he had spoken with a publisher, he neglected to supply a single line of manuscript copy. Lewis knew that his failure to publish the expedition's journals annoyed Thomas Jefferson.

There is evidence that Lewis became addicted to alcohol. Alcoholism might explain his failure to function efficiently.

On September 4, 1809, Lewis set out for Washington, D.C., carrying vouchers to justify his expenses as governor. He also brought along his journal, probably hoping to have it published. On the way, he stayed at Fort Pickering (near present-day Memphis, Tennessee). Captain Russell, the post commander, noted that Lewis was "in a state of mental derangement." Russell learned from boatmen who transported Lewis that Lewis had tried to commit suicide twice.[1] Lewis recovered his wits after five days, and rested at the fort for another ten days before leaving. The post commander believed that Lewis had a drinking problem.

On October 11, 1809, Lewis stopped overnight at a cabin called Grinder's Inn, on the Natchez Trail in the Tennessee wilderness. Late at night, Lewis staggered out of his room, wounded by two gunshots, one in his head, the other in his side. He died three hours later.

Neighbors of Grinder's Inn suspected that he was robbed and murdered, for their area was notorious for violent crime. Thomas Jefferson believed that mental depression caused Lewis to commit suicide. Leading scholars are now convinced that Meriwether Lewis killed himself.[2]

William Clark was well suited to his new responsibilities. Shortly after his return from the expedition he moved to St. Louis, where he successfully took over his duties as Brigadier General of the Militia for the Louisiana Territory.

THE INCREDIBLE JOURNEY OF LEWIS & CLARK

He was also delighted to serve as Superintendent of Indian Affairs, a post he enjoyed for life.

Because of his deep-seated concern about Indians' welfare, chiefs respected and trusted him. During the War of 1812, Clark was able to keep the Indians from being influenced by British agents, who had tried to incite them against the United States.

Clark was appointed Governor of the Missouri Territory three times. He held that post until Missouri became a state in 1820.

Clark married in 1809, raised a family of five (the first-born named Meriwether Lewis Clark), and volunteered to act as guardian for several Indian children. He died at the age of sixty-eight, in 1838.

York, who had been a valuable member of the expedition, was not given his freedom for many years. It is shocking to learn that Clark leased York to a man who misused him, and it is heartrending to know that York was married to a woman who was owned by another family. When Clark finally made York a free man some time before 1832, he gave his former slave a wagon and horses and set him up in business hauling freight. Clark was later told that York died of cholera, after years of drudgery.

Sacagawea and Charbonneau lived among the Mandans for a time. Their son, Jean Baptiste (Pomp), and a daughter of Charbonneau from another wife were brought to Clark, who acted as their guardian and arranged for their education in St. Louis. When **Jean Baptiste** grew up he became a well-known guide for western travelers.

Eventually Charbonneau and Sacagawea separated. He

spent the rest of his life guiding fur traders and acting as their interpreter.

No one knows how or where Sacagawea spent her remaining years. There are conflicting accounts about her death. According to a biography written by Grace Hebard in 1933, Sacagawea died at a Shoshoni Indian reservation in 1884. But according to a trader's journal, dated December 20, 1812, "this Evening the Wife of Charbonneau, a Snake [Shoshoni] Squaw, died of putrid fever she was a good and the best Women in the fort, aged abt 25 years she left a fine infant girl." Clark wrote that by 1828 Sacagawea was dead. Most historians have concluded that she died at an early age.[3]

Chief Big White (Sheheke), who joined the conquering heroes when they were welcomed in Washington, was a celebrity in the capital city. An enthusiastic public referred to him and his wife as "King and Queen of the Mandans."

Although he was fascinated by city life and enjoyed banquets, White House receptions, and tours of other cities, he was anxious to return to his people.

In 1807, Ensign Nathaniel Pryor (formerly Sergeant) was in charge of escorting Big White back to the Mandans. But the Arikaras attacked Pryor's boat, and the party was forced to turn back. The government did not again make arrangements to return Big White until 1809, when it paid the St. Louis Missouri Fur Company $7,000 to guarantee the chief's safe trip home. At least 120 armed men were employed to take Big White back to his people. The chief had been away for three years.

Big White was dismayed by the Mandans' reaction to his adventures. When he recounted his experiences, they called him "a bag of lies," and when he wore a United States military uniform, they mocked him. Big White was "no great warrior" in their eyes.[4]

THE INCREDIBLE JOURNEY OF LEWIS & CLARK

Little is known about the lives of most of the other men on the expedition. Some, like **Sergeant Patrick Gass, Sergeant Nathaniel Pryor,** and **Private Joseph Whitehouse,** reenlisted in the army. Others, like **Sergeant John Ordway,** married and settled on farms. **Private John Colter,** who became a fur trapper, gained fame as the discoverer of the Yellowstone Park area. **George Drouillard,** the expedition's expert hunter and interpreter, and **Private John Potts** also returned to the wilderness as fur trappers. They were killed by Blackfeet Indians in 1810.

Notes

Chapter 1: Top Secret

1. Mackenzie's route to the Pacific was too difficult to be used for trade. His book, *Voyages from Montreal,* was published in 1801, read by Jefferson in 1803, and carried as a reference book by the Lewis and Clark Expedition.
2. Donald Jackson, ed., *Letters of the Lewis and Clark Expedition with Related Documents 1783–1854* (Urbana: University of Illinois Press, 1962), Message to Congress, No. 8, 10–14.
3. Ibid., Message to Congress, No. 8, 10–14.

Chapter 2: An Intelligent Officer

1. The President measured and recorded rainfall, temperature, and wind direction; described the migrations of birds; noted the dates that plants flowered and had fruits; jotted down the times he noticed a new insect, a fresh leaf, spring's first frog croak, summer's first firefly, and autumn's last-heard katydid.
2. Dr. Rush might have been dismayed to learn that the explorers didn't take time out during the day for two-hour naps, that they would not think of soaking their feet in liquor that the group preferred to drink, and that they didn't eat sparingly in order to have energy.
3. Rush asked if Indian ceremonies were like those of the Jews. This question was included because many people believed that Indians were descended from the Lost Tribes of Israel.
    See Jackson, *Letters of the Lewis and Clark Expedition,* Benjamin Rush to Lewis, No. 8, 50.
4. Ibid., Jefferson's Instructions to Lewis, No. 47, 61.
5. The Louisiana Territory is equal to about one-third the area of the United States today (excluding Alaska and Hawaii).
6. See Jackson, *Letters of the Lewis and Clark Expedition,* Clark to Lewis, No. 74, 110.

Chapter 3: Getting Ready

1. See Jackson, *Letters of the Lewis and Clark Expedition,* Nemesio Salcedo to Pedro Cevallos, No. 119, 183–189.

2. A year later, one hundred Spanish soldiers set out from Santa Fe, New Mexico, but attacking Indians forced them to retreat. At any rate, they could not catch "Mr. Merry," who had already reached the Columbia River. Lewis was not aware of Spain's plot against him.

3. The legend of the lost Welsh tribe persisted until the 1950s.

4. Patrick Gass, *A Journal of the Voyages and Travels of a Corps of Discovery,* edited by David McKeehan (Minneapolis: Ross and Haines, 1958), 12.

5. Joseph Whitehouse, *Journal.* See Reuben Gold Thwaites, ed., *Original Journals of the Lewis and Clark Expedition* (New York: Dodd, Mead & Co., 1904–5), vol. 7, 30.

CHAPTER 4: THE VOYAGE BEGINS

1. Meriwether Lewis, *The Expedition of Lewis and Clark* (Ann Arbor: University Microfilms, Inc., 1966), vol. 1, 2. The nine young men from Kentucky were: Charles Floyd, Nathaniel Pryor, William Bratton, John Colter, Reuben Field, Joseph Field, George Gibson, George Shannon, and John Shields.

2. Sergeant Floyd died August 20, 1804, three months after the expedition started. His life could not have been saved even by the best doctors, since the first appendectomy wasn't performed until 1887.

3. The name is Seaman, not Scannon. See Donald Jackson, "Call Him a Good Old Dog, But Don't Call Him Scannon," *We Proceeded On* (August 1985), 5–8.

CHAPTER 5: THE FIRST POWWOW

1. See Thwaites, *Original Journals,* vol. 1, 97.

2. See Jackson, *Letters of the Lewis and Clark Expedition,* Lewis and Clark to the Oto Indians, No. 129, 203–208.

3. Paul Russell Cutright, *Lewis and Clark: Pioneering Naturalists* (Urbana: University of Illinois Press, 1969), 68.

CHAPTER 6: EXCURSIONS

1. See Thwaites, *Original Journals,* vol. 1, 119.

2. Ibid., vol. 1, 117.

3. The explorers subsequently saw thousands of pelicans nesting on a sandbar. The American white pelican is a species that breeds near rivers and lakes in the West.

4. See Cutright, *Lewis and Clark: Pioneering Naturalists,* 81.

CHAPTER 7: FRIENDLY INDIANS

1. See Jackson, *Letters of the Lewis and Clark Expedition,* Jefferson to Lewis, No. 105, 165–166.

2. See Thwaites, *Original Journals,* vol. 1, 129.

3. John Bakeless, *Lewis and Clark: Partners in Discovery* (New York: William Morrow & Co., 1947), 127.

4. Sergeant John Ordway, *The Journal of Captain Meriwether Lewis and Sergeant John Ordway, Kept on the Expedition of Western Exploration 1803–6* (Madison: Historical Society of Wisconsin, 1916), 120.

5. Several tribes are called *Sioux,* a name indicating that they speak the Sioux language. Sioux Indians are also called *Dakotas.*

CHAPTER 8: A TROUBLESOME TRIBE

1. James P. Ronda, *Lewis and Clark among the Indians* (Lincoln: University of Nebraska Press, 1984), 28.
2. See Thwaites, *Original Journals* vol. 1, 165.
3. See Ronda, *Lewis and Clark among the Indians,* 33.

CHAPTER 9: REFUGEES

1. See Thwaites, *Original Journals,* vol. 1, 188.

CHAPTER 10: WINTER AMONG INDIANS

1. See Ordway, *Journal,* 174.
2. Sacagawea's bravery and lovable qualities have made her a heroine of many books that falsify her role. Sacagawea did not act as guide, and she did not point the way. Most of the West was as new to her as it was to the explorers.
3. See Ordway, *Journal,* 175.
4. See Gass, *Journal,* 81–82.
5. Ibid., 87.
6. Lewis and Clark did not see the most important ceremony, the Okipa, a four-day rite involving self-torture. Men skewered the flesh of their backs or chests with hooks, and hung from a sacred pole until pain made them unconscious or caused them to have visions. The Okipa was performed before or after a summer buffalo hunt. Torture and fasting were tests of endurance and means of obtaining visions, which were interpreted as holy revelations. Lewis and Clark probably heard about the Okipa. They must have noticed scars on Indians' bodies. And they probably saw or heard of men who fasted to experience visions.
7. See Ordway, *Journal.* See Thwaites, *Original Journals,* volume 7, 174.
8. Ibid., 174.
9. See Thwaites, *Original Journals,* vol. 1, 243.
10. See Jackson, *Letters of the Lewis and Clark Expedition,* Lewis to Jefferson, No. 149, 231–236.

CHAPTER 11: JOURNEY INTO THE UNKNOWN

1. The permanent party (those who crossed the continent) was composed of:

Commanding:	Captain Meriwether Lewis
	Lieutenant William Clark
Sergeants:	John Ordway
	Nathaniel Pryor
	Patrick Gass
Interpreters:	George Drouillard
	Toussaint Charbonneau

Privates:		
	William Bratton	Baptiste Lepage
	John Collins	Hugh McNeal
	John Colter	John Potts
	Pierre Cruzatte	George Shannon
	Joseph Field	John Shields
	Reuben Field	John B. Thompson
	Robert Frazer	William Werner
	George Gibson	Joseph Whitehouse
	Silas Goodrich	Alexander Willard
	Hugh Hall	Richard Windsor
	Thomas P. Howard	Peter Wiser
	Francois Labiche	

York, Sacagawea, and her child Jean Baptiste Charbonneau accompanied the permanent party. (This list does not include those soldiers and rivermen who returned to St. Louis at the end of the Mandan stay.)

2. See Thwaites, *Original Journals,* vol. 1, 284–285.
3. Ibid., vol. 2, 20.
4. Ibid., vol. 1, 373. Grizzlies were not a newly discovered species. Explorer Alexander Mackenzie and other adventurers had encountered the animals before Lewis and Clark saw them.
5. See Jackson, *Letters of Lewis and Clark Expedition,* Lewis to Henry Dearborn, No. 236, 369.
6. See Thwaites, *Original Journals,* vol. 2, 15.
7. Ibid., vol. 2, 149. Power installations have destroyed this beautiful spectacle. The Great Falls were in present-day western Montana.

CHAPTER 12: FINDING SHOSHONIS

1. The other branches were named the Madison River, in honor of the Secretary of State, James Madison, and the Gallatin River, for the Secretary of the Treasury, Albert Gallatin.
2. See Thwaites, *Original Journals,* vol. 2, 340.
3. Ibid., vol. 2, 350.
4. See Lewis, *The Expedition of Lewis and Clark,* vol. 1, 382.
5. See Thwaites, *Original Journals,* vol. 2, 383.
6. Ibid., vol. 2, 381.

CHAPTER 13: FLATHEADS AND PIERCED NOSES

1. Sign language for Flathead: press both hands against the head in a flattening motion. This tribe did not flatten their heads. There *were* Indian tribes who flattened heads, but they lived farther west.
2. See Thwaites, *Original Journals,* vol. 3, 30.
3. Ibid., vol. 7, 150–151.
4. Gass, *Journal,* 164.
5. Sign language for Pierced-Nose Indians: pass the forefinger beneath the nose.

CHAPTER 14: RUSH TO THE PACIFIC

1. The Clatsops were a Chinook tribe.

CHAPTER 15: HOMEWARD BOUND

1. See Thwaites, *Original Journals,* vol. 4, 267.
2. Ibid., vol. 4, 267–268.
3. Ibid., vol. 4, 269.
4. Ibid., vol. 4, 343.
5. Clark realized his lack of qualifications as a physician. He apologetically explained, "We take care in many cases can administer and give such medicine and surgical aid as will effectually restore them in simple cases." See Ronda, *Lewis and Clark among the Indians,* 230.
6. See Thwaites, *Original Journals,* vol. 5, 52.
7. Ibid., vol. 5, 142.
8. Ibid., vol. 5, 217.
9. Ibid., vol. 5, 225.

CHAPTER 16: BACK TO CIVILIZATION

1. See Thwaites, *Original Journals,* vol. 5, 339.
2. Ibid., vol. 5, 343.
3. Ibid., vol. 5, 344.
4. See Jackson, *Letters of the Lewis and Clark Expedition,* Jefferson to the Arikaras, No. 198, 306.
5. See Thwaites, *Original Journals,* vol. 5, 371.
6. Ibid., vol. 5, 387.
7. See Jackson, *Letters of the Lewis and Clark Expedition,* Lewis to Jefferson, No. 207, 319.
8. Ibid., Jefferson to Lewis, No. 220, 350.
9. Ibid., Jefferson's Annual Message to Congress, No. 222, 352.

AFTERMATH

1. See Jackson, *Letters of the Lewis and Clark Expedition,* Statement of Gilbert C. Russell, 573–575.
2. Paul Russell Cutright, "Rest, Rest, Perturbed Spirit," *We Proceeded On* (March 1986), 7–16.
3. See Jackson, *Letters of the Lewis and Clark Expedition,* see note p. 639.
4. Herman J. Viola, *Diplomats in Buckskins* (Washington, D.C.: Smithsonian Institution Press, 1981), 90.

About the Illustrations

Several artists of the early nineteenth century have enabled us to visualize western landscapes and American Indians as Lewis and Clark saw them. George Catlin was the first important artist to travel through the Plains. During the 1830s he visited more than forty Indian tribes to depict their way of life. In 1833 Prince Maximilian of Germany employed Karl Bodmer as an artist to document his private Missouri River expedition. Alfred Jacob Miller traveled through the western wilderness in 1838, making hundreds of sketches of people and scenery. Indians of the Pacific Northwest were accurately portrayed by Paul Kane, who visited coastal tribes between 1845 and 1848.

These artists showed the land in its pristine beauty and left wonderful eyewitness records of tribal customs and ceremonies of the past.

The illustrations were selected by Rhoda Blumberg.

ACKNOWLEDGMENTS: Illustrations on pages 44 (top), 75, 122 (top), and 125 (bottom) courtesy of the Academy of Natural Sciences of Philadelphia; page 36 courtesy of the American Kennel *Gazette;* pages 44 (bottom), 45, 47, 48–49, 52, 67, 78, 101, and 119 courtesy of the American Museum of Natural History, Department of Library Services; pages 31, 41, 107, 108, 121, 123, 124 (top and middle), and 126 courtesy of the American Philosophical Society, Philadelphia; pages 82–83 and 113 courtesy of the Amon Carter Museum of Western Art, Fort Worth, Texas; page 33 courtesy of the Beinecke Rare Book and Manuscript Library, Yale University; page 20 courtesy of the College of Physicians of Philadelphia; page 87 courtesy of the Free Library of Philadelphia, Rare Book Department; page 85 courtesy of the Huntington Art Collection, San Marino, California; page 16 courtesy of the James Jerome Hill Library, St. Paul, Minnesota; pages 12, 18, 24, 58, 61, 70–71, 73, and 77 courtesy of the Library of Congress; pages 35, 95, 100, 122 (bottom), 124 (bottom), and 125 (top) courtesy of the Missouri Historical Society, St. Louis; pages 59, 89, and 94–95 courtesy of the Montana Historical Society Library, Helena; page 54 courtesy of the Museum of the American Indian, Heye Foundation, New York; page 19 courtesy of the Mutter Museum, Philadelphia; pages 8, 21, 28, 30, 38 (left and right), 56, 57, 62–63, 64, and 117 (left) courtesy of the National Museum of American Art, Smithsonian Institution; page 91 courtesy of the New-York Historical Society; pages 39, 51, and 79 courtesy of the New York Public Library, Astor, Lenox and Tilden Foundations; pages 29 and 42–43 courtesy of the Oregon Historical Society, Portland; pages 96, 99, 102–103, and 104–105 courtesy of the Royal Ontario Museum, Toronto; title page, 15, 27, 46, 81, 88, 97, and 117 (right) courtesy of Walters Art Gallery, Baltimore. ILLUSTRATION CREDITS: Illustrations on pages 61, 70–71, 73, 77, and 119 by Karl Bodmer (1809–1893); pages 8, 21, 28, 38 (left and right), 51, 56, 57, 62–63, 64, 67, 79, and 117 (left) by George Catlin (1796–1872); pages 96, 99, 102–103, and 104–105 by Paul Kane (1810–1871); pages 30 and 95 by Charles B. King (1785–1862); title page, 46, 81, and 88 by Alfred Jacob Miller (1810–1874); page 89 by Edgar Paxson (1852–1919); pages 18, 24, and 31 by Charles Willson Peale (1741–1827); pages 59, 94–95, and 113 by Charles M. Russell (1864–1926); pages 91 and 121 by Charles B.J.F. de St. Mémin (1770–1852); pages 82–83 by Charles Wimar (1828–1862).

Bibliography

Allen, John Logan. *Passage through the Garden: Lewis and Clark and the Image of the American Northwest.* Urbana: University of Illinois Press, 1975.

Bakeless, John. *Lewis and Clark: Partners in Discovery.* New York: William Morrow & Co., 1947.

Cutright, Paul Russell. "I gave him barks and saltpeter." *American Heritage* 15, December, 1963.

——. *Lewis and Clark: Pioneering Naturalists.* Urbana: University of Illinois Press, 1969.

DeVoto, Bernard. *The Course of Empire.* Boston: Houghton Mifflin Co., 1952.

——, ed. *The Journals of Lewis and Clark.* Boston: Houghton Mifflin Co., 1953.

Dillon, Richard H. *Meriwether Lewis: A Biography.* New York: Coward-McCann, Inc., 1965.

Gass, Patrick. *A Journal of the Voyages and Travels of a Corps of Discovery.* Edited by David McKeehan. Minneapolis: Ross and Haines, 1958.

Gray, Ralph. "Following the Trail of Lewis and Clark." *National Geographic Magazine* 103, June, 1953.

Hawke, David F. *Those Tremendous Mountains: The Story of the Lewis and Clark Expedition.* New York: W. W. Norton & Co., 1980.

Jackson, Donald, ed. *Letters of the Lewis and Clark Expedition with Related Documents 1783–1854.* Urbana: University of Illinois Press, 1962.

——. *Thomas Jefferson and the Stony Mountains.* Urbana: University of Illinois Press, 1981.

Jefferson, Thomas. *Notes on the State of Virginia.* Boston: Lilly and Wait, 1832.

Josephy, Alvin M., Jr. *The Nez Perce Indians and the Opening of the Northwest.* New Haven: Yale University Press, 1965.

Malone, Dumas. *Jefferson and His Time.* Vol. 3, *Jefferson and the Ordeal of Liberty.* Boston: Little Brown and Co., 1962.

Martin, Edwin. *Thomas Jefferson: Scientist.* New York: H. Schuman, 1952.

Lewis, Meriwether. *The Expedition of Lewis and Clark.* Vol. 1. March of America Facsimile Series, no. 56. Ann Arbor: University Microfilms, Inc., 1966.

Meyer, Roy W. *The Village Indians of the Upper Missouri.* Lincoln: University of Nebraska Press, 1977.

Olmsted, George W. *Fielding's Lewis and Clark Trail.* New York: William Morrow & Co., 1986.

Ordway, Sergeant John. *The Journal of Captain Meriwether Lewis and Sergeant John Ordway, Kept on the Expedition of Western Exploration 1803–6.* Madison: Historical Society of Wisconsin, 1916.

Ronda, James P. *Lewis and Clark among the Indians.* Lincoln: University of Nebraska Press, 1984.

Spencer, Robert F., Jesse P. Jennings, et al. *The Native Americans.* New York: Harper & Row, 1977.

Thwaites, Reuben Gold, ed. *Original Journals of the Lewis and Clark Expedition.* 8 vols. New York: Dodd, Mead & Co., 1904–5.

Viola, Herman, J., *Diplomats in Buckskins.* Washington, D.C.: Smithsonian Institution Press, 1981.

We Proceeded On. The Official Publication of the Lewis & Clark Trail Heritage Foundation.

Index

THE INCREDIBLE JOURNEY OF LEWIS & CLARK

Rhoda Blumberg

is acclaimed for her informative and compelling books for young readers. Her previous book for Lothrop, *Commodore Perry in the Land of the Shogun,* received a Newbery Honor, a Golden Kite Award, and a Boston Globe–Horn Book Award, among other important honors. The *Bulletin of the Center for Children's Books* called it "a book with reference use that reads almost like an adventure story."

A native of Brooklyn and a magna cum laude graduate of Adelphi College, Ms. Blumberg worked as a radio script writer and a journalist before writing books for children full time.

Rhoda Blumberg lives on a farm in Westchester County, New York.